Deep Health

ALSO BY

BRIAN LENAHAN

Artificial Intelligence: Foundations for Business Leaders and
Consultants

Digital Coach: Coaching in the Era of Artificial Intelligence

Artificial Intelligence: Transitions – How to Prepare for a Career
Where AI is Everywhere

Deep Health

**Using Artificial Intelligence to Live Longer
and Healthier**

Brian T. Lenahan & Rob Kowal

**Aquitaine Innovation Advisors
Toronto**

Deep Health Copyright © 2020 by Aquitaine Innovation Advisors. All rights reserved. Printed in the United States of America. For information, address Aquitaine Innovation Advisors publishing.

www.aquitaineinnovationadvisors.com

Designed by Brian T. Lenahan & Rob Kowal
Co-publishers: Aquitaine Innovation Advisors, Kriscor & Associates

Library of Congress Cataloging-in-Publication Data
Names: Lenahan, Brian T., 1963- author; Kowal, Robert W., 1958- author.
Title: Deep Health – Using Artificial Intelligence to Live Longer and Healthier / Brian Lenahan, Robert Kowal
Description: First edition. | Toronto: Aquitaine Innovation Advisors, 2020. | Includes bibliographical references and index.
Identifiers: ISBN 978-1-989478-08-0 (paperback) | ISBN 978-1-989478-09-7 (ebook)
Subjects: LCSH: Human-machine systems. | Artificial Intelligence. | Automation.

Cover design: Brian Lenahan & Kristin Kowal

Our books may be purchased in bulk for promotional, educational, or business use. Please contact your local bookseller, through www.Amazon.ca or by email at
www.aquitaineinnovationadvisors.com

First Edition: September 2020

10 9 8 7 6 5 4 3 2 1

Publisher's Note

Every care has been taken to ensure the accuracy of the information provided in this book. However, it is sold with the understanding that the publisher and authors are not engaged in rendering professional services. The information in this book is not intended to diagnose or treat any individual's health problems or ailments. The information given is not medical advice and is not intended to provide a course of personalised treatment. The publisher, the author, or their respective employees or agents shall not accept responsibility for injury, loss or damage to any person acting or refraining from action as a result of material in this book whether or not such an injury, loss or damage is in any way due to negligent act or omission, breach of duty or default on the part of the publisher, the author or their respective agents. There may be risks involved with some of the natural ingredients identified in this book. If professional advice or other expert assistance is required, the services of a competent health practitioner should be sought.

Software and hardware vendors and their products noted in this book are in no way endorsed or sponsored by the authors or publisher, rather are included as directional information for the reader.

Aquitaine Innovation Advisors
Kriscor & Associates

Dedication & Acknowledgements

For those open to benefitting from our experiences to live longer and healthier lives using artificial intelligence; for those who represent hope and love; and for those who find the power inside to overcome the barriers life puts in front of them - Brian

This book is dedicated to those striving to achieve optimal health & wellness.
To Teresa, Kristin and Courtney for your encouragement, love and support - Rob

Acknowledgements

We would like to thank our editors for keeping us on track and providing their insights and recommendations, Deb Hanrahan, Karen Kelly, Courtney Kowal, Brad McKay, and Geralyn Ochab. We also extend our appreciation for the marketing support of Jennifer Mercieca, Samantha Cox and Kristin Kowal without whom the world of online advertising would not be so easily understood. Wherever we go, we talk about Deep Health and the opportunities for humanity in the future so, we would like to thank those we encounter who keep us even more inspired on our journey.

Table of Contents

Why This Book and Why Now?

"Take care of your body. It's the only place you have to live."
– Jim Rohn

Writing a book is no easy task. So why are we doing this? It's because of where we're at in our health and fitness journeys today and because we're excited about how Artificial Intelligence is increasingly converging with the Internet of Things creating the potential to positively impact your life. We're so excited to share our journeys.

Throughout this book, we will highlight some of the existing technologies and peek into what the next-generation technologies will look like. There is no better time to understand the world of artificial intelligence than now, especially when AI is being applied to the world's most pressing problems like climate change, traffic flow, disabilities, hunger, vaccine research and healthcare.

In the simplest terms, artificial intelligence is the attempt to have computers mimic human thought and action. However, there is nothing simple about the effort to make that happen. Our brains have billions of cells and, combined with our synapse connections, outnumber stars in the universe. The evolution of AI has been slow. However, AI has evolved to the point that it can mimic speech, hear, see, move, and more.

From the perspective of your health, AI has the potential to change and improve your life significantly. In ***Deep Health***, we share our ideas, experiences and research to help you become more aware of your unique health status. We introduce you to the concepts of biological age, the Internet of Bodies (IoB), predictive health, Digital Twin and our *Deep Health* model, and to the incredible experts providing thought leadership in this field. Not to mention introducing you to early adopters of AI in the health and fitness domain. We are confident that smart technology powered by artificial intelligence will provide you and your health care providers with the information you need to make better choices about the food you eat, your fitness level, and your mental health.

Regardless of which stage you are at in life, we hope that by reading this book, you will see the potential in the new technology and think differently about AI and how it can help you hyper-personalize your health and wellness. Take the time to learn about AI's capabilities. Take the time to make a difference in your nutrition, your fitness, and your health. Your future is out there; artificial intelligence can help guide you on your way.

Rob Kowal and Brian T. Lenahan

Introduction

"Health is like money, we never have a true idea of its value until we lose it." – Josh Billings

Brian joined our Starbucks weekend coffee group (affectionately known as the "genius bar") in the summer of 2016. When we met, I could tell Brian was a typical stressed-out executive (it takes one to know one!). He was employed by a top 10 financial institution in a high stress and demanding position. The signs of his declining health were visible. Brian was very overweight and showed in his facial features, and as I would learn, he had high blood pressure (HBP) and developed type 2 (T2) diabetes. The years of stress from extensive corporate travel, eating fast food on the go, drinking and eating late into the evenings, lack of sleep and little or no exercise, not to mention contributing to his family and raising two children had taken a toll.

By early 2017, Brian had had enough and retired at a young age of 53. Brian's health was suffering, and he was searching for answers and committed to improving his health. As we got to know each other, I shared my corporate experiences as a food industry executive (I have a background in food science and technology) and my passion for nutrition and health. I shared my health challenges, including my weight loss issues and the big wakeup call in my life after being diagnosed and surviving prostate cancer.

The revelations about our health status were shocking for both of us. Brian was only 53, technically obese with HBP and T2 diabetes. I was overweight and had prostate cancer (PC) at 56! We both were looking for answers, and the information from our doctors was not good enough! My doctors told me that all men are at risk of getting prostate cancer, and the older you get, the higher the chance. Statistically, 1 in 7 men gets the disease and 1 in 27 dies from it. I was told it's just part of ageing.

Maybe genetics plays a role? No one in my family had a history of PC. Maybe lifestyle and diet? Both Brian and I started looking for answers. It had to be something that we were doing or not doing. Like many in our age group, we had gained a lot of weight. At my peak, I weighed 230 lbs with a 40" waist. Brian was 220 lbs with a 38" waist. I was classified as Obese Class 1 (BMI of 31), and Brian was the same (BMI of 30). I was told that I carried the weight well because of my height (6"1"), but I started to feel sluggish, lacked energy, had sore joints and experienced 'foggy' brain.

My research helped me learn about the causes of chronic disease prevalent in Western society (obesity, T2 Diabetes, cardiometabolic disease and some cancers). It was then I found research about the consumption of dairy and the possible link to prostate cancer. For most of my adult years I was a big consumer of dairy products. Could this be the cause of my cancer?

As we got to know each other, it became apparent that Brian and I had a lot in common, and our interests overlapped. Brian is passionate about the exponential growth of technology, big data, Artificial Intelligence, and its impact on businesses. I am passionate about health and nutrition and its effects on society.

Brian realized that early retirement is not for everyone, and to remain engaged and channel his energy; he enrolled in MIT to learn more about Artificial Intelligence. The majority of our conversations often revolved around health and lifestyle. As Brian progressed through his MIT education, he would often interject stories about the explosive growth of AI and how technological innovation would rapidly change the way we work and live. Brian has since turned this passion into three published books on the subject. Before long, it became apparent that our mutual interests would intersect, and we started to write about the convergence of technology with health and wellness.

I wanted to do everything I could to keep prostate cancer at bay, and after radical prostatectomy, I am five years clear. I changed my diet. Eliminating wheat and dairy products made a huge difference. Sore joints, acid reflux and foggy brain disappeared. My weight dropped 20 lbs in 45 days. I started to exercise more and took up road cycling. I am now down 40 pounds from my peak weight.

Brian has also taken control of his health, lost 30 pounds, and has his type 2 diabetes under control through lifestyle and diet changes. Adult-onset diabetes affects millions of us, and indeed, in Brian's case, it was linked to a lifestyle of a poor diet, stress, and lack of exercise. Brian wanted to rid himself of diabetes, or in medical terms, send it into remission (a Weill Cornell Medicine-Qatar study found that a year-long intensive program focused on lifestyle rather than medication, sent 61% of participants into remission). So, he investigated how AI could help him achieve that goal. This book is the result of that year's long investigation.

Our journey so far has brought us to this point. We are passionate about learning more and taking control of our health and extending our health spans (my personal goal is to live to a "healthy" 100 or longer). We are excited about the role AI and big data will play in helping us live longer and healthier lives. In this book, we will share insights and compelling data about how to gather information and start to take control of your health.

Ageing and health decline are not inevitable. What if we could gain a deeper understanding of the connection between diet, exercise, lifestyle and an extended health span? To understand this and give you more context, let's explore the current landscape.

SECTION 1   YOUR HEALTH & AI

Chapter 1

The Disaster Zone

"Getting older doesn't have to mean degenerating health and diminishing energy. You can enjoy prime-of-life vitality and cut years from your age." – Longevity Magazine

We are not alone with our health challenges. 69% of Canadian adults and two-thirds of Americans are overweight or obese. We know that obesity is linked to many chronic diseases, including high blood pressure, T2 Diabetes, and even some cancers. The cost to society for health care and the burden on our families is staggering. What we refer to as the 'Disaster Zone'.

According to a 2017 report from the House of Commons Canada, "It is estimated that chronic disease and other illnesses cost the Canadian economy $190 B annually with $122 B in indirect income and productivity losses and $68 B in direct health care costs!" In the USA, the numbers are even more staggering. In 2016, direct healthcare treatment for chronic health conditions totalled $1.1 trillion (6% of US GDP).

In 2017 there were 56 million deaths globally. Of that, 31 million deaths were due to mostly preventable non-communicable diseases, including cardiovascular diseases, cancers, diabetes, respiratory diseases, and kidney disease. In contrast, according to OurWorldinData.org & Institute for Health Metrics and Evaluation (IHME), since 1990, deaths by injury are virtually unchanged at 7% of the total to 2017. Communicable, maternal, neonatal and nutritional diseases have declined from 35% to 20% of deaths.

Starvation versus Obesity

People are often surprised when they hear about the global ratio of overweight people to those undernourished. As of March 2nd, 2020, there were 841,244,953 undernourished people in the world. By contrast, there were 1,689,806,952 overweight people in the world. A ratio of 2:1. Of those classified as overweight, 751,379,258 people are classified as obese.

On any given day, over 10,000 people succumb to hunger. In the United States, $191,000,000 is spent daily on obesity-related (preventable) diseases, and consumers spend over $63,000,000 annually on weight loss programs. An incredible dichotomy in this shared world.

Adults are not the only age group suffering from obesity. In fact, according to the US Center for Disease Control data, approximately 18% or 13 million youths globally are obese. Obesity is defined by the CDC as a body mass index (BMI) at or above the 95th percentile of the CDC sex-specific BMI-for-age growth charts.

Our current "healthcare" system is lacking. It's often referred to as our "sick care" system. Don't take this the wrong way; we need and are thankful for our highly skilled doctors and nurses, especially when it comes to traumatic injury or if we need a sophisticated surgery that could potentially save our lives (like Rob's prostate cancer surgery). Doctors are highly trained and competent in these areas.

However, many doctors are in what Dr Mark Hyman, Director of Cleveland Clinic Center for Functional Medicine, has coined the "name it, blame it, and tame it" game when it comes to chronic disease. Through no fault of their own, doctors are not trained to look for the root cause of chronic disease. Do you have high BP? Here is a pill to tame it. Do you have type 2 diabetes? Take a pill, and if it gets worse, take some insulin. Cardiovascular disease? Depression? IBS? – there is a medicine for that (more on this in Chapter 3).

Almost all chronic diseases are related to poor lifestyle choices, such as smoking, the food we eat, lack of physical activity, lack of sleep, stress etc. What we eat is a leading factor. Consumption of too many refined carbs, sugars and industrial fats, combined with a sedentary lifestyle, is a formula for disaster.

According to Dr. Hyman, the future of medicine is personalized treatment, not "one-size-fits-all." The outdated method of naming the disease and then assigning a drug to fix it clearly isn't working.

The common mantra we hear about obese people are things like, "you're lazy, and you overeat." But it is not necessarily your fault. We eat what we have easy access to. Most of us don't cook fresh foods (who has time?). We have easy access to take-out meals, drive-thru coffee and muffins.

For most of us, poor health is a slow decline. Many are inadequately prepared or even know anything about preventing these diseases and don't find out about it until something goes wrong. Most of us understand that we need to make changes to our diets and exercise more, but this is often an overwhelming task. So much information is available. Whom do we listen to? What information is fact and what is fiction? What diets work? What should I eat? The list goes on.

In early 2020, we wrote an article captioned, "It's GOOD for you!... It's NOT GOOD for you!" We asked the question, 'What should you eat?' Over the decades, we'd heard conflicting information about coffee, eggs, bacon, wine and other foods. The articles about these foods all start with "a new study has found..." contradicting a series of other studies from different sources.

How do you sort through this information and choose ideal foods for you, your physiology, and your stage of life? We are exposed to so much information about what to eat and what to avoid. How can we know what is fact and what is fiction? How can we possibly absorb and analyze all this data? What if we could collect and assess all this data to determine the ideal food choices for you? Not for the masses, or for men versus women, or seniors. A perfect diet specifically for YOU.

There are hundreds of existing diet programs, and they vary in terms of their effectiveness (Atkins, Keto, Paleo, South Beach, Mediterranean, Zone, vegan, and vegetarian to name a few). According to Market Research.com, in 2018, the total U.S weight loss industry had grown to $72 billion and continues to grow at an annual rate of about 4% a year. Many of these diets and programs work for some, but not all, because they are not customized for your unique physiology. If they do work, they are often not sustainable or affordable.

We all have different genomes (the complete set of genes or genetic material present in a cell or organism) and physiological differences, so what we eat will affect each of us differently. Imagine being able to tap into our DNA sequence and your microbiome (the microorganisms in and on your body) and customize a diet program to optimize your health! This is not a future dream. The technology exists today.

Companies exist where you submit an oral swab test (*'23 and Me'*) or a stool sample (*Viome*) for analysis. The samples are assessed and, and then by leveraging their AI algorithms, they can evaluate the thousands of data points to tell you what diseases you might be predisposed to, what you should eat and what you should avoid.

So how will the pursuit of health through food choices change in the future? One word. Data. Lots of data being analyzed using artificial intelligence. Being able to gather and analyze massive amounts of personal data will change how you perceive yourself and help you make personalized choices to optimize your food selection, consumption and lifestyle habits.

Chapter 2

Life Expectancy

"Time and health are two precious assets that we don't recognize and appreciate until they have been depleted." - Denis Waitley

In just 100 years, life expectancy around the world has doubled. Over 600 million people, or 8.5% of the world population, are over the age of 65! In the next 30 years, this same age group is forecast to double, those over 80will triple, and one in five will be over 60. Estimates from the AARP (American Association of Retired Persons) suggest half of those older than 65 will require long-term care.

The US Census Bureau forecasts that over the next 40 years, the population of centenarians (people 100 years and older) will increase from 10,000 to almost 600,000. According to a report from Statista, by 2100, North America's median age will increase to 46 from 30 in 1950.

The ten nations with the oldest populations, according to the Global Agenda Council on Ageing, those countries with the highest percentage of people over the age of 60, namely Japan, Italy, Germany, Finland, Sweden, Bulgaria, Greece, Portugal, Croatia and the UK's Channel Islands.

There is no doubt that globally most countries citizens are living longer, but are we living healthier? As shown in the chart below, in Canada, 44% of adults over 20 have at least 1 of 10 Chronic (and preventable) conditions:

Hypertension	Osteoarthritis	Mood/Anxiety Disorder	Osteoporosis	Diabetes
25%	14%	13%	12%	11%
Asthma	COPD	Ischemic Heart Disease	Cancer	Dementia
11%	10%	8%	8%	7%

In 2014, 18 million or three in five Canadians said they felt they had very good health. By 2018 that number had grown to 19 million or 60% of the entire country. Yet 10 million reported they had a BMI that would be considered overweight, and 7 million reported being obese.

These numbers are staggering and, in my (Rob) opinion, are getting worse. Having watched my 84-year-old mother die from colon cancer complications, hooked up to a respirator, unconscious and with no hope of ever recovering was very difficult for me and has motivated me to remain as healthy as possible for as long as I can. I believe that good health can become a mindset!

There are plenty of examples of people in their 70's, 80's and 90's who are bucking the statistics and are still healthy and contributing to society. Octogenarian's like actors Patrick Stewart (Captain Picard of Star Trek fame) 80; Clint Eastwood is still producing movies at 89; Judi Dench - 85 and Maggie Smith - 85.

There are plenty of other examples like Mick Jagger (76), Warren Buffet (90), and our local politician and former Mayor of the City of Mississauga Hazel McCallion (98). Getting older doesn't mean we need to fade away into poor health or spending our final years in long term care.

Longevity

When I (Brian) first retired in 2017, I gave a great deal of thought about the next stage of life. How long and healthy might my life be? My grandparents and parents lived well into their nineties. Odds are, I will too. With such a long possible runway left ahead, I started to consider how I could optimize my remaining time. The first step was to increase the likelihood of living that long by improving my health.

During my research, I started to learn how regular exercise affects our epigenome, activating genes that improve things like muscle function. The more I exercised, even when I started by getting off the couch and walking half a block, the better I felt, and I could sense my brain feeling sharper and more active. Even though I was in my early fifties, I decided it was not too late to start.

Fortunately, because I didn't smoke and steered clear of those who did, my lungs were in reasonable shape, and I wasn't affected by any of the potential side effects of long-term smoking. Unfortunately, living longer is not merely the absence of diseases; it's also healthy living, which I was not doing.

I was among the millions of people who love the taste of potatoes, especially french fries. Before my shifting health focus, I would have a version of potatoes for breakfast, lunch and dinner (hash browns, potato chips, and traditional fries). I could blame my Irish-Canadian background for these cravings, but each time it was still my choice. The food choices that I made, exacerbated by high stress, missed meals, and corporate travel combined to form the perfect storm resulting in high blood pressure, cholesterol and diabetes. This was the basis on which I became determined to live longer. I was really behind the starting line. But I started anyway.

One of the most daunting diseases I faced was diabetes. To understand the impact of diabetes on aging, we constructed the graph below. In essence, if you have advanced type 2 diabetes and are not taking insulin of any kind, your body is jeopardized in managing blood glucose levels and the inherent impacts on your body. By taking insulin, your body can more readily maintain healthy blood- glucose levels. By adopting a natural lifestyle, including balanced nutrition and exercise, one can improve blood glucose to more normal levels whether or not healthcare practitioners recommend insulin. Part of living longer is attacking disease with natural tactics.

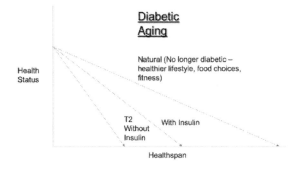

Source: Brian Lenahan

People like Rob and me over the age of 50 are the fastest-growing demographic group worldwide. Many of us will live into our 80's or longer. Like Rob, I want to live a long life and extend my health span for as long as possible. Today, there are plenty of examples of countries or regions where this takes place. Author Dan Buettner refers to these areas in his book, The Blue Zones. Dan points to locations like Okinawa, Japan; Loma Linda, California; Sardinia, Italy;

Nicoya, Costa Rica; and Ikaria, Greece, where a high percentage of the population are centenarians and are still healthy!

The elderly population in Japan in the 1860s was just a few percent, in 2020, it's more than a quarter of the population. Within 40 years, that number is predicted to exceed 38%, retaining the top spot globally. One expert from the University of Tokyo, Dr. Hiroko Akiyama, when collecting data on the elderly, found that one's health at age 65 is highly correlated with "quality of life for the rest of life," which becomes increasingly important when considering a possible 100-year lifespan. Diet plays an essential role in how these centenarians age. However, there are also many social and environmental factors at play. Being socially active, maintaining independence, and having a close-knit family unit, contributes to good mental health and a strong support network during stressful events.

The world's population is about to encounter a significant shift. In 1950, India's population was 380 million. By 2100 it is projected to be 1.45 billion, similar to today's Chinese population, which according to some predictions, will decline significantly to 1.06 billion.

According to Our World in Data, "in 2018, the number of people older than 64 years old surpassed the number of children under five years old" for the first time. Life expectancy increases are due to "an increase in healthcare expenditure [where] the proportional highest gains are achieved in poor countries with low baseline levels of spending," thus the India experience. In the United States, while healthcare spending is higher than any other nation, and interest in longevity is surging globally, life expectancy is declining. Research published in the Journal of the American Medical Association determined that while life expectancy increased for 60 years in the US since 2014, it has declined. Some point to societal issues (i.e. drugs, suicide); others point to health issues like diabetes, Alzheimer's and cardiovascular issues being amongst the most expensive. Add them all up. According to the Milken Institute, as of 2016, the price tag of chronic diseases is $3.7 trillion (or about $10,000 per US citizen) in the US alone or approximately 20% of Gross Domestic Product (GDP).

Today, there is an entire 'longevity industry' for products and services devoted to living longer, generating trillions of dollars. The United Kingdom, with over 10 million retirees, has over 250 companies, a dozen non-profits, and ten research labs today to support that industry. Globally, the longevity economy consumes up to 20% of GDP or $17 trillion US as of 2019, growing by 50% by 2026.

As part of the World Economic Forum, the Global Future Council on Longevity seeks to heighten awareness of longevity and health-based activities through systemic change. It is just one such organization. The US National Academy of Medicine holds a 'Health Longevity Global Grand Challenge.' We are hopeful these organizations succeed in getting their message of healthy longevity out to a global public that needs such guidance.

Society is being transformed by investments, government policies, and consumer spending on efforts to live longer. As humans healthily extend their lifespan and research is augmented by artificial intelligence, our actions can be enlightened. As more robust data, AI, faster processing and research talent converge, new medical advances are expected to become available in the science of aging, personalized diagnostics, and 'agetech'. Agetech includes mobile apps for the elderly, continuing education, and cognitive enhancement.

Geroscience, or the science of understanding how the aging process enable diseases, includes rejuvenation biotech, regenerative medicine, gene therapy and nutraceuticals. Age can be thought about in several ways, and in the next section, we will look at the difference between chronological age and biological age.

Chronological Age vs Biological Age

When we think about age, we logically think about our chronological age. The days, months and years on the calendar. But that isn't the only way to think about it. We're sure you have heard or used the phrase "I feel older than my age, or "I feel younger than my peers". After three years of committed exercise and food choice changes, I (Brian) feel as young as I did 20 years ago. I can run as fast and as far. I can lift the same weights. I can recover from strenuous exercise as quickly. I weigh only a few pounds more. All measurable facts. So how does that translate in terms of my real age?

When we considered people in our age group, we observed widely varying states of health. Those observations were for many reasons, which we discuss below, but they bolstered our view that not all humans were the same simply because of our chronological age or the period from when we were born to today. So we wondered, 'how could we measure the difference between the calendar and how we felt physically and mentally.' In part, because we wanted to celebrate the progress we both had made, but also to inspire others to think about their age differently. That different measure is one's 'biological' age.

Biological age (also called physiological age) takes many lifestyle factors into account, including your environment, diet, sleep and exercise pattern and physiology to determine how your body is ageing. One tool to calculate your biological age is not surprisingly called **biological-age.com**. A myriad of factors goes into the tools' assessment. (we will share the main categories below and a full listing in the appendices of this book). So much more than just a turn of the calendar.

Year born	Happiness level
Where you live (country)	Number of friends
Gender	Breakfast frequency
Education level	Hydration level – Number of Glasses of Water
Body Shape	Servings of Fruit and Vegetables
Hours of sleep daily	Frequency of eating deep-fried/refined foods
Alcohol consumption	Personal diet (vegetarian, lean meat, everything)
Stress levels	Cholesterol level
Physical activity frequency	Number of pushups
Strength training frequency	Relation description (ie happy, supportive)
Medical checkups	Enjoy your vacations?
Dental checkups	Smoking frequency
Blood pressure	

According to another tool, ***RealAge,*** which covers many of the same factors, suggests Rob, who is chronologically 62, has a biological age of 36. From the same assessment, Brian, who is 57, has a biological age of 31.

Factors in Biological Age	
Age	Employment status
Height	Education level

Weight	Family Income
Blood Pressure	Sleep duration
Cholesterol	Major Stressors
HDL	Financial Stress
Personal opinion on Health	Social partnerships
Health problems	Do you like your life?
Asthma?	Where you live
Diabetes?	Encouragement from others on health
Tobacco use	Encouragement from others on energy
Second-hand smoke	Learning new things every day
Alcohol use	Improving the area where you live
Aspirin intake	Feeling active/productive
Cancers?	Speed of walking
Heart-attack?	Time doing aerobic exercise
Stroke?	Time doing weight training
Therapy for depression	Time sitting per day
Chronic pain	Servings of fruit
Dental Visits	Servings of vegetables
Colon Cancer Check	Servings of dairy
Flu Vaccine	Soda consumption
Pneumonia Shot	Servings of nuts
Medication for Mood	How much processed food
Taking Medication as	How much vitamin D

Prescribed	
Keeping Medical appointments	How often you wear a seat belt
Relationship status	Does the vehicle have airbags
Relationship happiness	Do you smoke
Number of people in household	Ethnic background

How much thought do you give to these factors every day? Would your biological age change as a result? While the age derived from these tools are directional, the above list from *RealAge*, for example, does not include genetics, blood type, resting heart rate, recovery rate, REM vs deep sleep data specifically.

Optimum Span

We've spoken above about your lifespan, which includes health and longevity. However, that's not all there is to life. What about your happiness? Few would choose to live a long but miserable life. So, when we refer to longevity and healthspan, we mean to infer that people generally want to be happy in concert with those elements. There are numerous sources to cite when it comes to living a happy life, and we defer to those resources when deciding upon actions directed at making you happier. We are very interested in the concept of not just lifespan or healthspan but something we call "optimum span." Optimum span includes health, longevity, and happiness, and we wish it most fervently upon all of you.

Chapter 3

Your Food & Current Dietary Advice

"If we could give every individual the right amount of nourishment and exercise, not too little and not too much, we would have the safest way to health". - Hippocrates

Most of us know that a healthy, nutrient-rich diet is essential for living healthier and longer lives. It protects you from many chronic diseases such as heart disease, diabetes and some cancers. For many of us, knowing what foods to eat and what supplements to take can be challenging.

As mentioned in Chapter 1, many medical doctors receive minimal nutrition education. Even if they did, they rarely have the time to discuss and identify how your diet and lifestyle affect your health or cause your illness. According to the American Heart Association (AHA), medical schools may have gaps in nutrition education. Without adequate instruction during residency or earlier medical school segments, healthcare practitioners focus on a somewhat limited perspective as an AHA science advisory found in the April 30, 2018 edition of *Circulation*. "Any nutrition education gained is likely to be lost if not reinforced and translated into practical how-to knowledge," the advisory authors wrote.

Dr. David Eisenberg, director of culinary nutrition at the Harvard T.H. Chan School of Public Health, agreed with the AHA advisory. Eisenberg stated the advisory documents "the total lack of requirement in most medical schools to understand the practical skills necessary to advise patients struggling with their weight, blood sugar, blood pressure or heart disease."

At best, most of the dietary advice we get, especially from our doctors, is very generic. Cut back on our fat (if you have high cholesterol), sugar (if you have diabetes), and salt (if you have high blood pressure). While situations and circumstances vary, many medical doctors are more likely to prescribe medication before trying to identify the root cause of the disorder and advise on how to correct this without it.

Many diet programs are designed around the calories in/calories out model and are solely to help people lose weight. These programs are well-meaning and work for some, but according to a study published in the British Medical Journal, "most diets, regardless of which one, lead to weight loss and lower blood pressure, but these desired effects largely disappear after a year".

There is much more to health than just weight loss. It is difficult for most of us to know what to eat, how much to consume, and whether we are getting the required nutrients. Western diets, especially fast food, consist of salt, fat and sugar and rarely have enough of (if any) the complex micronutrients we need to sustain and optimize our health.

Access to these cheap, fast foods has never been easier. We can now order any meal quickly and easily with our smartphone. Many of the "fast food" chains use delivery services like Uber Eats. In early

2020, the most popular takeout orders delivered by Uber Eats in 35 U.S. states were fast foods. Topping the list in six states were french fries, followed by other variation of fries (spiced, etc.) appearing in five states, chicken varieties topped demand in another five states, Pad Thai in four, burritos and nachos in three. Pennsylvanians apparently love their cheesesteak.

Sugary foods are ubiquitous, cheap and easy to access. Sugar is often referred to as "white death." Dr. Robert Lustig, UCSF Professor of Pediatrics in the division of Endocrinology, is a big proponent of banning sugary foods. He argues that the damage from the consumption of too much added sugars (especially fructose), and insufficient dietary fibre, plays a significant role in the obesity epidemic.

So how do we educate and navigate around these dietary challenges? What goes into determining and optimizing the ideal but unique, personalized and customized diet and lifestyle for individual consumers? How can someone collect and make sense of all that data?

Let's dig deeper into food choice. Today, it's possible to collect data on macro and micronutrients, including vitamins, minerals, and carbohydrate intake. To measure your food selections' nutritional value, consumers can scan the nutrition label using an application like *Foodnoms* instead of manually entering it. Scanning nutrition labels is an easy way to incorporate this information into your decision-making process.

Applications like *Ava, CalorieMama* and *BiteAI* use food image recognition to collect food nutrition data. If you're counting calories, *FitGenie, MyFitnessPal* and food logs, such as *Yazio* are existing applications consumers can use. If you are into intermittent fasting (discussed later in the book), applications like *Zero* are available to coach you through this.

Preferences

Some food may be good for you, but your taste buds may not agree with you. Food preferences should be considered in the overall personal data analysis. Let's face it if the food doesn't taste good; we may not consume it, even if it's good for us (brussel sprouts anyone?). When analyzing data, taste must be considered, because if the consumers' taste buds' rebel, or if it conflicts with their morals (like eating meat), then the AI recommendations won't fly.

Brian and I regularly talk about how exponential growth in technology is changing our lives. We always learn something new about the impact of food choice, exercise, and emerging technologies on our health and lifespan.

AI will be able to combine all of the data mentioned above into personalized recipes just for you. "MIT's Computer Science and Artificial Intelligence Laboratory (CSAIL), working with the Qatar Computing Research Institute and Universitat Politecnica de Catalunya, developed *Pic2Recipe*, an AI system that creates recipes from pictures of food. The artificial neural network (ANN) reads more than a million recipes and finds patterns between ingredients and the images. *Pic2Recipe* was largely successful but needs further refinement when evaluating pictures of food containing many different ingredients, such as lasagna. As the technology is refined, neural networks such as *Pic2Recipe* will help consumers know what is in their food and the exact amount of each ingredient. Such an advancement could be of considerable significance to those with allergies or those trying to adhere to very specific diets.

Software like Nutrino's *FoodPrint* combines various sources of information to uncover "the invisible connections between people and food to empower better nutritional decisions for better health outcomes." The application incorporates data science, predictive analytics, natural language processing, optimization theory, and predictive analytics to support food selection. *Nutrino* is one of many companies leveraging AI to map out personal optimized diets or supply food characteristic analysis. Others include *Zipongo*, *Eat This Much*, *FiNC*, *Lose It!*, *Nutritionix, Validic* and *Omada Health*.

The *Smart For*k is a device you can use to self-monitor eating habits and help you to slow eating motions. By tracking hand speed and the time between bites, the *Smart Fork* alerts you through vibration and a red light, whether you're eating too fast.

Another health-focused app is EWG's *Healthy Living* app, a smartphone app that gives red, yellow, and green indicators on select foods like cereals. If carcinogens, allergens or toxins are your concern, one option might be the *Think Dirty* app, which can be used while shopping for items like underarm deodorant or shampoo.

Nima is billed as the "world's first portable gluten detector" for people concerned about (celiac disease) or are allergic to gluten. *6SensorLabs* of San Francisco developed a pocket-sized sensor which offers one-time test capsules, allowing the user to track and share data.

Blood Type Diet app is based on the diet developed in the mid-1990's by Peter D'Adamo centred on an individual's blood type. This has become very popular, and many believe longer, healthier lives are possible through food choices aligned to their blood type. Combining the impact of blood type into food choices can be meaningful to anyone focused on a healthier life.

Supplements

Rob highly recommends nutritional supplements. Much of the food we consume is devoid of the necessary macro and micronutrients our bodies need to function at optimal levels. Rob's daily supplements include a high-quality bioavailable multivitamin and mineral supplement, 1200 IU of Vitamin D, 1500 mg of Glucosamine, 1500 mg Vitamin C, 1200 mg of Omega-3, 500 mg of Turmeric (curcumin) and 500 mg of Resveratrol.

We are both fans of Resveratrol. In scientific terms, it's a "stilbene and non-flavonoid polyphenol" produced by various plants, including grapes and blueberries. Resveratrol's' antioxidant, anti-inflammatory, anti-carcinogenic properties are said to protect your heart and is anti-mutagenic. We often hear that resveratrol can be found in a glass of wine, though insufficient quantities to be useful. It also limits platelet aggregation, which refers to how well your platelets clump together to form blood clots. Yet advice varies, and we remind the reader that every person's physiology is different.

Dr. David Sinclair is an Australian biologist and professor of genetics best known for his research on anti-aging. He and other experts suggest that resveratrol, available in supplement form at most nutrition stores, combined with other supplements, shows promise as an anti-aging agent because of its anti-inflammatory and antioxidant properties.

According to the Council for Responsible Nutrition, about 75 percent of Americans consume dietary supplements. Yet, 40% of those do not review their choices with their doctor or health care provider before consuming them. Despite their popularity, supplements remain unregulated.

Pharmacologic is the branch of medicine concerned with the uses, effects, and modes of action of drugs, including traditional drugs and dietary and herbal supplements. The latter is less well represented in pharmaceutical databases, and less information is available to the public, especially concerning their potential interactions (contraindications). Prescriptions can be interfered with as can over-the-counter medications. In the past, no tool existed for consumers to gain insights into the risks associated with supplements. How can you be sure a supplement, like Resveratrol, is safe for you to consume?

Supp.ai, developed by the Allen Institute for AI (a non-profit organization), is a database of over 2,000 supplements, over 2,700 drugs and almost 60,000 interactions. The model used by *Supp.ai* extracts data from over 20 million papers from the U.S. National Institutes of Health search engine called PubMed and lists evidence of supplement-drug interactions and supplement-supplement interactions. It's free and maintained and verified by the Institute on an ongoing basis. *Supp.ai* developers cite a disclaimer that the information in the database does not replace a qualified or licensed physician's advice. Good advice, to be sure, but also understand that many physicians know relatively little about nutritional supplements and, as previously mentioned, have very little training in nutrition and holistic health.

The *Supp.ai* application is an example of the incredible capabilities of artificial intelligence when applied to supplements. AI provides doctors, naturopaths, holistic nutritionists, and other healthcare practitioners access to data that has been sorted and analyzed and offers insights and recommendations, in this case, about how prescription medications and supplements interact.

As a health care practitioner using artificial intelligence within your practice to expand and personalize a patient's nutrition or treatment program offers the opportunity to analyze massive amounts of information, including combinations of vitamins and nutrients, to provide personalized, optimized treatment or dietary recommendations. Both patients and doctors can now access such data, to refine nutrition programs or pharmaceutical treatments, and reduce the risk of adverse reactions when prescribing supplement regimens.

Vitamins, Minerals and AI

An excellent example of how AI can help us optimize our supplement choices is Vitamin D. This vitamin is sometimes referred to as the "sunshine vitamin" because it is produced in your skin in response to sunlight exposure and has several essential functions like helping boost your immune system. We also know that Vitamin D affects bone mass, bone quality, and helps regulate mood. Many of us, especially in the Northern Hemisphere, do not get enough sunlight and are probably lacking sufficient levels. Normal blood serum levels for adults range from 50 – 100 micrograms per deciliter. Because we may not be getting enough sun exposure, especially during the winter months, we need to supplement. The recommended level for adults is 500-600 IU per day. But how do we know how much we actually need? Each of us is so unique that standardize dose recommendations of 500 IU might be sufficient for one person and woefully too low for another.

Until recently, the only way to find out your vitamin D level was to ask your doctor to test for this specifically. This may not be part of their standard procedure. If you go to a functional medicine doctor or naturopath, they may check this as part of their routine diagnostic practice. However, these tests will require a blood sample and analysis from a reputable laboratory. There are home test kits available from companies like *Visymo*; however, they still require a finger prick test and the need to wait up to 5 days to see results.

In the not too distant future, we imagine that a home test will be available to analyze and provide your results instantly. The results will link to your smartphone and add to your health database. In the near future, an implantable chip will most certainly measure Vitamin D, amongst many other vitamin and mineral metrics on a 24/7 basis.

One Student's Approach to Nutrition Apps

Jennifer Mercieca is a Commerce graduate from McMaster University in Hamilton, Ontario, Canada. Jennifer is like many of her peers in that she leverages her smartphone for fitness and nutrition purposes. She uses *Lifesum*, a free version software app, to scan foods and barcodes and help to track and manage her daily calorie intake and nutrition. She uses the free version of Lifesum because as a student, funds are often not available, so free versions are a great way to manage until a post-education period. Jennifer focuses on foods that help her achieve her goals.

Jennifer monitors how much she eats in terms of number and type of calories, carbohydrates vs protein vs fat calories, and more to augment her fitness regime. The self-advertised "digital self-care app that helps you reach your health and weight goals through better eating." Jennifer's use of the app depends to some extent on how busy her schedule is. While it is relatively convenient to add in the food log or snap food photos (5-10 minutes max per day), it's not always done if life gets busy.

Jennifer selected the app based on reviews and ratings and downloaded it from one of the app stores. One of the app's downsides is that homemade foods can't easily be tracked in terms of caloric content (amount and type). Even entering ingredients one-by-one, some portions don't fit within the app. She creates her unique recipes and saves them for future reference and also refers to some of the app's recipes.

Jennifer discusses the app results with her friends and peers to gain further insights from other users of similar apps and how they apply that information to their fitness routine. She says if it wasn't for others' influence, she might not have been as motivated to get to where she is today.

Steph Marcil, skier and former member of the Canadian National Ski Team, and AI enthusiast, embraces the world of nutrition and its impact on the human body. "AI will be the most powerful tool in the field of nutrition. No longer will we rely on population studies to create nutrition guidelines. Every individual will have a personalized nutrition strategy towards achieving optimal health. Wearables and implants will quantify important factors such as blood glucose levels, nutrient status, hormone levels and stress markers, and our AI nutritionist will be able to analyze these metrics and provide real time feedback for improvement. The ability to predict the outcome of our dietary choices will not only allow us to achieve our health goals but also prevent disease. AI will give us the power not only to understand who we are, but more importantly how we can become the person we want to be." With innovators like Steph, we're confident that the combination of artificial intelligence and nutrition are in good hands.

Chapter 4

Collecting Data

"These technologies can make life easier, can let us touch people we might not otherwise… These things can profoundly influence life."
— Steve Jobs

Dr. Donald W Milne, a 66-year old anesthesiologist with the Antelope Valley Hospital in California, owes his life to the Apple Watch. Detecting an otherwise unknown heart condition, Dr. Milne found that he required corrective surgery. While detecting atrial fibrillation is a known feature of the popular wearable, this story illustrates how the Apple Watch can detect heart disease even within someone who had no prior history of it.

While doing an elliptical workout, Milne experienced greater than usual shortness of breath, so he consulted the ECG function on his Apple Watch. An indicator called ST-segment depression appeared on the tracing, which returned to normal with rest. Appointments with his primary physician and a cardiologist determined that Milne had critical diffuse coronary artery disease, resulting in a follow-up surgery for a "5-vessel bypass and aortic valve replacement". Milne went on to say, "without the Apple Watch tracing; I would never have known I had the disease in time to be able to intervene before having a potentially fatal heart attack."

In October 2019, James Prudenciano fell down a cliff while out hiking with his date in Hartshorne Woods Park in New Jersey. According to the news report, "Prudenciano fell into the river and landed on a rock. He suffered three fractures in his back."

Prudenciano continued "There was no way out of this for me. I literally said my last goodbyes". Fortunately for Prudenciano, Apple Watch has a "fall detection" feature that called 911 and directed emergency services to his location using the watch GPS feature.

Rob had a similar experience when he fell while out riding solo in the "middle of nowhere" in Ontario, Canada. Although not injured, his watch detected the fall and immediately displayed a notification. If Rob did not respond within one minute, emergency services would have been notified and dispatched to his location. Rob is comforted to know that if anything should happen while out riding in remote areas, that his watch, as it did for Dr. Milne and James Prudenciano, could save his life.

As the above examples illustrate, the value of wearable technology is becoming more evident daily. There are more and more stories about how smartwatch technology is saving lives and helping us live healthier. In this chapter, we discuss many forms of wearable devices and smart technology that can be used to collect data, whether to safeguard your life or simply get fit.

The umbrella term "smart technology" refers to electronic devices that collect digital data through physical sensors incorporated into a watch, phone, implant, or lens. Such devices either transmit the data to another device or store the data and complete the computations themselves.

The Pew Research Center conducted a survey in 2019, which found that 20% of North Americans wore a smartwatch or fitness tracker. Globally, 6% of the world's population (442 million people) are wearable users, according to Statista, a statistical research company. During the April to June period of 2020, various brands collected revenue in North America of $2 billion with Apple at 38% of the market and Fitbit at 19%.

By tracking users' heart rate, sleep patterns, blood pressure, the number of steps, body mass index, and weight, and trending that data in graphic format, wearable devices have progressed to be incredible data generators. The full potential has yet to be realized.

Smart clothing is an exciting departure for wearable devices. High tech outerwear, embedded with numerous sensors, including pants, shirts, jackets, gloves and more, are being created by manufacturers worldwide with estimated sales of $5.3 billion by 2024 (from $1.9 billion in 2019) according to MarketsandMarkets.com.

In certain parts of the world, mask-wearing is commonplace. In 2020, due to COVID-19, we are now seeing this almost everywhere. In a crisis like this, human ingenuity always surfaces. *BioScarf* is an N95 rated air filtration device. The fashionable scarf reduces respiratory health risk, including pollutants, allergens and viruses.

Montreal-based *Hexoskin* smart shirts collects data about the wearer's heart rate, heart rate variability, electrocardiogram, heart rate recovery, breathing rate, activity intensity, acceleration, cadence, steps, positions and more. The wearer can download their data to a paired phone or tablet and analyse through Open Data API. In terms of health research, cardiology, pulmonology, neurology, paediatrics, and psychiatry researchers can leverage the *Hexoskin* data.

From the *Deep Health* perspective (the authors view of this whole world), smart technology users can apply early detection and intervention into their health programs either solo or in conjunction with their healthcare practitioners. Smart technology personalizes your data and compares it to a broader population, providing personal insights and a more global perspective. For example, Brian's Samsung Active Watch compares his fitness activity to others in his age group (did he mention he is in the top 6%?).

Sensors are an intrinsic part of the smart device, and increasingly new advanced technologies like smart pills, robotic surgeries, and holographic simulations, will have an increasing impact on human health.

The Internet of Bodies

There are many reasons why consumers are turning to digital technology for healthcare. People use digital capabilities to search for doctors, doctor reviews and ratings, healthcare plans, and hospital ratings. They also perform prescription refills, check on personal health information and make payments. Yet one of the most interesting phenomenon is how our bodies are getting connected to the internet.

The fuel for AI is data. Generally speaking, the larger the dataset the better. When it comes to our health the vast dataset can be collected in a variety of ways. The interconnection of everyday devices is referred to as the Internet of Things (IoT).

The Internet of Bodies (IoB), an extension of IoT, will collect huge amounts of data from external, internal, and embedded devices. Rather than devices connected to the internet, IoT, human bodies can be connected to networks, being remotely monitored and in some instances, controlled.

Think of your body as a new data discovery ecosystem. Smart toothbrushes, digital pills or ingestible sensors, and virtual rehabilitation programs form part of the new IoB environment. Sharing data to support medical studies or one-on-one with your trainer, your body creates trillions of data points that can be mined through the Internet of Bodies to optimize your health.

Gesture Controls

Have you ever thought about using your smartwatch without touching the watch? You can do that today with gesture control. Gesture control is, according to Gartner, "the ability to recognize and interpret movements of the human body to interact with and control a computer system without direct physical contact." The **Mudra Band** (Sanskrit for ritual hand gesture), for example, "slides over your Apple Watch screen just like a normal band, and instantly turns the watch into a single-handed device." The sensors in the band allow the user to use simple finger and hand gestures to control many features on the watch, like answering or hanging up a call, moving forward on a screen, or controlling your music. Answering a call by clenching and unclenching your fist forms part of the new feature package of the Samsung Galaxy Watch 3.

The preceding description is the simple version, but how do gesture controls work from a technology perspective? Electrodes in the watchband identify the neural signals sent from your brain, through your wrist to your fingers, and AI algorithms (deep learning) deciphers the signal pattern and tells the watch which finger moved and in which direction which operates a function on the smartwatch. That kind of fits into the "what will they think of next" category doesn't it? While running, walking, or carrying bags, your hands are free to control your wearable devise. All in the name of convenience.

Self-tracking

With the explosion in wearables and the associated data, people learn a great deal more about themselves than they ever could before. Other related terms are auto-analytics, self-surveillance, and body-hacking, where people gather data about their sleep patterns, fitness activities, food choices, DNA and more.

Consider the case of instrumentation in the modern car. When you see the 'Check Engine' light come on in your vehicle, you need to react to the alert or diagnosis. Diagnostics are performed very differently than in the past. My father was a mechanic, and he relied largely on his own senses to assess a car's performance. Mechanics today depend on computers to analyse sensor data provided onboard like brake wear, tire pressure, engine performance, fluid levels, and more. Some of today's cars have over 200 sensors. Each self-tracking sensor provides millions of data points that need to be analyzed to optimize the vehicles' performance. So too with the human body. The data from you can be transferred electronically to central locations in the cloud or shared with your medical practitioner.

Transferring Information

Wearable devices will provide your doctor with both static and real-time data and the robust data interaction between doctor and patient will become routine. Presently, Apple Watch provides EKG information that a cardiac patient can send to their cardiologist. Future Apple Watch iterations will feature live feed updates and the built-in pulse oximeter (already part of the watch, but not approved yet for use) will provide blood oxygen levels. Early warnings of a problem will alarm the patient and doctor, potentially saving countless lives. The same built-in oximeter and HR monitor will allow professional athletes to read real-time data to access their performance on the go, sending their coaches up to the second updates.

Brian and I love our smartwatches, and we track hundreds of data points daily. Those of us who exercise regularly, or even weekend warriors will be able to monitor their results, and AI will analyze the data providing direction and help with customizing optimal workout and diet programs. This data is collected effortlessly and covers a wide range of categories, including:

- Activity
- Body Measurements
- Cycle Tracking
- Hearing
- Heart Rate, Heart Rate Variability, EGC
- Mindfulness
- Nutrition
- Respiratory, Sleep and Vitals.

Let's explore a few of these readings and what the smart technology can tell us.

Resting Heart Rate

Variations in heart rate can vary widely, and are influenced by age, fitness level, medications, illness and stress. To truly measure resting heart rate, the measurement should be taken under appropriate resting conditions and duration. Fitness should also be measured by heart rate during exercise, which can vary widely from start to peak.

Rob and I are in the same general age group. He is an avid cyclist and has a resting heart rate between 51 and 56 bpm. As a more moderate exerciser, my resting heart rate is between 55 and 60. Both are considered excellent for our ages. Target heart rate charts are available from many sources (including images on Google) for you to determine your optimal resting heart rate.

Wearable technology makes this easy and effortless to track. Smart watches monitor heart rate 24 hours a day and provide you with very accurate data. The newest Apple Watch (series 3 and up) can now take your ECG (approved by FDA and Health Canada). A quick 30-second measurement relays the data to your health app on your iPhone. You can then generate and send a pdf of your results directly to your doctor or cardiologist from your phone.

Heart Rate Variability (HRV)

HRV is a measure of the variation in the time interval between heartbeats. According to a 2018 study of literature by the National Institutes of Health, heart rate variability (what's happening between heartbeats) can be a determinant of stress. Individuals with higher HRV may have better cardiovascular fitness and be more resilient to stress.

Smartwatch heart rate sensors capture these beat-to-beat measurements. Because there are so many variables and data points for your unique health, artificial intelligence can be your partner to provide the insights you need. Wearables are an evolving data source to power that artificial intelligence.

VO2 Max

VO2 max or maximal oxygen consumption calculates your ability to use oxygen or said in another way, the maximum amount of oxygen your body can utilize when you exercise. A higher VO2 Max indicates a higher level of cardiovascular fitness and aerobic endurance. Rob's VO2 max is 41 and, for his age group (aged 60+), puts him in the "Excellent" category. (see the table of Vo2 Max Norms for Men below).

Age	Very Poor	Poor	Fair	Good	Excellent	Superior
13-19	<35.0	35.0-38.3	38.4-45.1	45.2-50.9	51.0-55.9	>55.9
20-29	<33.0	33.0-36.4	36.5-42.4	42.5-46.4	46.5-52.4	>52.4
30-39	<31.5	31.5-35.4	35.5-40.9	41.0-44.9	45.0-49.4	>49.4
40-49	<30.2	30.2-33.5	33.6-38.9	39.0-43.7	43.8-48.0	>48.0
50-59	<26.1	26.1-30.9	31.0-35.7	35.8-40.9	41.0-45.3	>45.3
60+	<20.5	20.5-26.0	26.1-32.2	32.3-36.4	36.5-44.2	>44.2

Bone Mass

Bone mass is the amount of a person's weight that is comprised of bone. Bone mass is estimated based on a person's gender, and weight, i.e. a male weighing 170 lbs would, on average, have a bone mass of 7.3lbs. Lack of bone mass can be an indicator of protein deficiency or osteoporosis. The scale can give you an approximate reading, but we always recommend getting a bone density test if you suspect a problem.

Collecting Data

Brian's earliest example of collecting data was shopping online for a new weigh scale. Measuring your weight is a simple thing. Every weigh scale can do that, and weight alone really doesn't tell you anything. What about measuring body fat, body mass index (BMI), muscle mass, visceral fat, bone mass and body water level? Until recently, if you wanted to know this information you had to request this from your health care provider or from your fitness instructor (if you have one). Now it's possible to accurately measure all these parameters in the comfort of your home. I was hoping to find something more advanced than a traditional weigh scale. Sure enough, I found many cost-effective hardware and software options. I selected the *Etekcity* Digital Weight Scale (under $40 US) and the accompanying *VeSyncFit* app (free in your app store). The scale syncs with your smartphone, and when you step on the scale, an electric pulse is directed through your body, providing not only your weight but the following 12 other data points as well:

1) Body Mass Index
2) Body Fat Percentage
3) Fat-free Body Weight
4) Subcutaneous fat (the fat under your skin)
5) Visceral fat (the fat around your organs)
6) Body Water Percentage
7) Skeletal Muscle Percentage

8) Muscle Mass

9) Bone Mass Percentage

10) Protein Percentage

11) Basal Metabolic Rate (minimum energy needed)

12) Metabolic age

Rob and I regularly assess what the 12 metrics from the weigh scale are telling us and adjust our eating habits and fine tune our fitness routines accordingly.

External wearables like smartwatches monitor certain aspects of our health like sleep patterns, heartbeat, VO2 max, exercise rates and trends. Internal devices like pacemakers help measure and regulate heart rate, and indigestible capsules with microchips will measure the composition and health of our microbiome. Embedded technology like subcutaneous microchips will provide in-depth, 24/7 analysis of our physiology through brain controller interfaces, which can emit brain signals to restore function to those with disabilities.

Collecting Data from a Smartwatch

Let's take, for example, the Apple Smartwatch 4 with the Apple Health App. The smartphone can be synched with your watch to identify 28 active measures, per the list below:

1) Active energy - calories burned over and above metabolic rate (natural sitting burn rate)

2) Blood Pressure – manually entered

3) Body Fat %

4) BMI

5) Caffeine levels

6) Cycling distance (any activity)

7) ECG (watch)

8) Environmental Sound levels (7-day exposure)

9) Exercise minutes

10) Flights of stairs climbed

11) Headphone audio levels

12) Heart rate (bpm)

13) Height

14) High Heart Rate Notifications

15) Low Heart Rate Notifications

16) Lean Body Mass

17) Mindful Minutes

18) Fall detection

19) Resting energy

20) Resting heart rate

21) Sleep analysis

22) Standing hours (i.e. every hour, for how long)

23) Number of steps taken

24) Swimming distance

25) V02 max

26) Water level (drinking)

27) Weight

28) Workout (duration of workout)

This amount of data can be overwhelming!

Rob and I share the detailed reports and graphs from the Apple Health and Samsung Health, respectively. We compare notes and gain some great insight from the watch's reports. These two embedded apps take us closer to the ***Deep Health*** environment we will describe in Chapter 13.

DNA Tests

Understanding your unique DNA as it relates to health and fitness is a relatively new phenomenon. The Human Genome DNA sequencing project was started in 1990 and completed in 2003 at the cost of $1 billion. The Human Genome DNA sequencing project mapped all 20,500 human genes, composed of 3 billion chemical base pairs. Scientists, DNA specialists and DNA firms now understand the structure of the DNA chain allowing for increasingly accurate assessment of your DNA and, in turn, things like personalized healthcare treatment plans.

The popularity of DNA testing has exploded globally, starting with just a handful of companies in 2013. The number of testing kits ordered by consumers worldwide doubled in 2019 alone to over 25 million. Indeed, the most popular reason for testing is ancestry (I found out about my Scandinavian ancestors! You can check out what Scandinavian countries are doing in AI in the Appendices). Yet increasingly consumers are ordering tests for health information.

What health information are we talking about? Each cell in your body holds approximately 728MB of data and creates 1.7MB of it per second (according to Domo's Data Never Sleeps 5.0 report). Through machine learning and deep learning, artificial intelligence, trained on and analysing the cell data, provides incredible insights.

DNA sequencing provides many opportunities for us. It identifies genetic risks and develops personalized treatment plans and even "fixes" genes (with obvious ethical considerations). CRISPR, or clustered regularly interspaced short palindromic repeats, is a family of

DNA sequences first described by Osaka University researcher Yoshizumi Ishino and his colleagues in 1987. CRISPR sequencing can be applied in the agriculture sector to create probiotic cultures, enhance crop yields, and immunize food cultures. From a human perspective, CRISPR is used to look for genetic mutations, electrochemical miRNA (mitochondrial RNA) diagnoses, and disease treatments. In July 2019, CRISPR technology successfully treated a 34-year old Tennessee woman with sickle cell disease.

When it comes to things like optimal food selection, your genetic disposition contributes a great deal. Companies like *Ancestry*, *MyHeritage*, and *23andme* gather DNA data from consumers for family history/genealogy and provide a better understanding of your predisposition to certain diseases or tendencies like aversion to certain foods (i.e. lactose or gluten intolerance).

Lifenome, a New York City-based company, assesses your DNA through a saliva sample to determine DNA variations and predispositions specific to you. Using AI, *Lifenome* can take vast amounts of data, re-run its models, and improve their assessment predictions. Such information can improve your lifestyle choices around nutrition, exercise, skin care, allergy and personality and potentially lead to greater longevity. *Lifenome* won the bronze medal for insurtech (insurance technology) at the Zurich Insurance Innovation World Championship, given its potential to save money for insurers through precision employee health and wellness.

The *'DNANudge'* band makes use of your DNA data as you shop for your groceries. When you scan food item barcodes, the band will display a green light (for good), red light (for not good), letting you know whether it's an acceptable food choice. It then posts recommendations to your smartphone for red light food alternatives.

The *DNANudge* band's inventor also created the microchip capable of reading a mouth swab sample, uploading the wristband's DNA profile in an hour rather than the traditional eight weeks. Over time, the cost will continue to decline as we see improvements in processing speeds, storage capabilities and artificial intelligence. Other vendors in the AI/DNA space include *Genomelink, Promethease, GEDmatch, Habit, DNAFit, Dot One, Sequencing.com, GeneBlueprint, and BioGeniq*.

Buyer Beware

There are many stories in the media about being wary of DNA tests and their results being fake or inaccurate. You can look to reviewers like *GeneticsDigest* (who recommend *CRIGenetics*, 23andme, and Ancestry DNA as their top 3). They look at company reputation, services offered, testing method, etc., and seek vendors with credible data security and a professional pedigree.

DNA tests can provide fascinating insights into your coffee consumption, diet choices, and propensities for specific activities like wine drinking, yet not all tests are created equal. When considering a DNA test, we recommend you consider the following 13 points:

1. Don't look for a "final" answer. DNA sequencing today is directional towards more in-depth analyses.
2. some vendors have fewer samples
3. or fewer results,
4. some don't take ethnicity into account,
5. some have much higher costs,
6. some bundle between heritage or health and diet,

7. some don't limit the transfer of information to your insurance company,

8. some are the equivalent of a clinical test or just for fun

9. some have tax benefits if under prescriptions

10. some permit existing tests to be reused by another vendor

11. some are not authorized by the FDA or other regulatory body

12. The test is only a single point in time (static DNA markers), vs. continuous testing (blood glucose, microbiome, cholesterol, post-antibiotics, gluten digestion, etc.).

13. In some cases, they are clinical tools for which insurance companies would cover the cost.

The world of DNA testing is fascinating and fast-evolving. As consumers of data, we're excited at the prospects for more hyper-personalized information, yet we are also cautious about the considerations we've raised in this chapter, so buyer beware.

Chapter 5

Fitness

"Exercise is king. Nutrition is queen. Put them together and you've got a kingdom".- Jack Lalanne

Staying active is critical if you want to live healthier, longer lives. According to the Mayo Clinic, most of us need a minimum of 150 minutes of moderate aerobic activity per week and strength training at least two times per week. According to research at the Cooper Clinic in Dallas TX, just 30 minutes of cardio three to five days a week can add six years to your life. Do that plus a couple of days of resistance training and you'll not only live longer but also look younger, feel happier, and have more energy.

However, most of us fall woefully short of getting enough exercise. Between 2010 and 2015, the CDC notes only 22.9% of U.S. adults between 18 and 64 met 2008 guidelines for both aerobic and muscle-strengthening exercise. According to Statistics Canada, only 16% of Canadian adults are getting the recommended amount of physical activity (150 minutes of moderate-to-vigorous physical activity per week). That means 84% of the adult population is not active enough. According to Eurostat, "while almost half (49.8%) of the population aged 18 or over in the European Union (EU) did not do any sport, almost a third (29.9%) spent at least two and a half hours per week of leisure time doing physical activities in 2014. This includes cycling as a form of transportation".

When we exercise, are we optimizing our workouts to get the most out of the time we spend? Are we overdoing it? Are we getting enough?

Smartwatches and other wearables like WHOOP allow us to capture a plethora of data that can help coach us to an optimal workout. Brian and I track all our data with our smartwatches and electronic smart scales. Wearable technology is booming and will continue to grow. According to an article by Alicia Phaneuf, Associate Content Marketing Producer, Business Insider, "wearable fitness technology has weaved itself into society so that Fitbits and smartwatches are seen as mainstream; and the future of wearable devices shows no sign of slowing down." The demand for wearable technology is expected to reach a market value of $57.6 billion by 2022 from $19.6 billion in 2016, rising during the forecast period with a significant compound annual growth rate of 16.2 percent.

As a teenager, American football was my (Brian's) sport. I was playing various positions on offence and defence as dictated by the coaching staff. I enjoyed the energy level of real game competition yet was restrained and bored by practice. It seemed training and practice were driven by repetition and generic exercises than by optimizing the individual. Each player followed the same regimen as a group regardless of physiology differences and how they performed in that

60

exercise. Group exercises benefited the overall team but failed to optimize individual performance.

In the age of artificial intelligence, tools to collect data are everywhere, and in the sports arena, it's no different. Sensors, algorithms, wearables, cameras, and fixed equipment are all 'in play.' They are available to the athlete of 2020 and are being used in a myriad of ways.

Some large organizations have already embraced fitness data trends. In 2019, Google offered to purchase Fitbit for $2.1 billion, and for a good reason. Fitbit's data. Imagine what the world's largest search company could mine from the Fitbit database. All this data can be collected via smartwatches today and shared with your health care provider contributing to a deeper understanding of your health.

Individual Athletes

Rob is an avid cyclist covering about 50 km per ride over undulating terrain and inclines of up to 15 percent. He trains most days, mapping out routes, distances, and elevations. Rob pushes himself to perform better every day at these elements. Yet this represents a small fraction of the data that Rob collects.

So, what role does artificial intelligence play in his cycling? In addition to the data collected by Rob's Wahoo Element Bolt GPS bike computer (e.g. distance, average speed, elevation gain, lap pace, cadence), there is a significant amount of data collected by his Apple Watch. Active and total Calories, average heart Rate (include maximum and minimum), heart rate recovery, heart rate variability, and even audio noise levels.

Weight training is another common fitness activity. Combining sensor technology and artificial intelligence can provide real-time feedback to optimize workout results and activities combined with, or in place of, interactions with coaches. Wearables in the form of clothing or watches embedded with sensors generate the data elements identified in Chapter 2, including the amount of exertion, strain and recovery (a **Whoop** band feature) and signal to the wearer that they should take some action.

For the athlete, leveraging data from gyroscopes, accelerometers, and heart rate monitors (previously undetectable metrics without a coaching or training facility) embedded in wearables can help them, and the coach identify inefficient training practices, mistakes, and movements inside a practice or game.

By drawing on a large population and individual data, machine learning can analyse the wearer's input, compare it to the average and provide insights in real-time. When I (Brian) wear my Samsung Active Watch 2, it shows me my pace and speed per kilometre, my heart rate, speaks the results out loud for me, and then compares me to others my age who are using the same watch type to tell me what ranking I have (top 6% - hurray!). Over time my watch gathers more and more trend data, and learns about my goals, my activities and rewards me with a colorful badge when I've met my goals. Combining my watch with my smartphone provides a more profound comprehension of my activities.

For coaches, having artificial intelligence capabilities can be a game-changer during practice and during a game. Augmenting wearable sensors with high-speed cameras and apps like *gameface.ai*, coaches can see in much greater detail the athlete's performance.

How has the combination of the COVID pandemic and advances in artificial intelligence altered people's view of going to the gym? Apparently, as a population, we are getting fit without our usual trips to the gym. With gyms being closed or restricted, or individuals being intimidated by other gym users or fear of infection on behalf of its patrons, people have explored alternatives, including working out at home with apps that are often AI-powered.

One survey conducted in July 2020 of 2,000 Americans found that 50% of those polled used fitness apps for the first time, while 56% believed they would not be returning to the gym. One such AI-powered app, *Freeletics*, is used in over 160 countries by over 45 million users. The app, free at the lowest tier, concentrates on activities using your bodyweight combining High-Intensity Training (HIT) and High-Intensity Interval Training (HIIT) methods. The app, which seeks to optimize your health, learns about you individually, ultimately designing a unique workout from a selection set of over 3.5 million different options. According to *Freeletics,* the AI scores a perfect rating on its suggestions 85% of the time. With input from human fitness experts, the recommendations consider your available gear, profile, and data from millions of other users and develop a personalized program.

Interview with a Boxer

Brittany Pequegnat is a bio-organic scientist, with a Ph.D. and an affinity for boxing. Her intriguing combination of pursuits motivated us to interview her recently. We asked her about her motivation in each of these pursuits. "My motivation for science and vaccines come from my passion for helping others. The knowledge that something I am passionate about being able to help another being to live more comfortably is my main driving force". Brittany continues, "Vaccines have the ability to prevent or get ahead of an illness, and they also have the ability to alleviate symptoms. It is their adaptability that makes them an interesting field, and also an inspiration to be adaptable in my life. Fitness and nutrition became increasingly important to me as I understood the importance of being well later in life. It's not about being able to lift heavy now, or fit into smaller clothing, but to be able to do things like simply carry groceries inside later in life. We have to put in the effort now while we can in order to reap the benefits later.

As a boxer my motivation comes from a different place, a feeling of being lost on my journey. I always had a common theme in my life - striving to meet the next goal. Upon leaving my post-doctoral position I found myself in a place I had never been before, a place where there was no clear next goal to achieve, no next challenge to put myself up against. After some time in a confusing place, I decided it was time to go outside my comfort zone and attempt a new challenge, and that happened to be by walking into a basement boxing gym, Back Bay Boxing, in Boston. The love grew from there, and upon returning to Toronto, I used this challenge to further grow as an athlete and push myself to new heights with the help of High Definition Performance Group. My continued motivation comes from the mindset that problem-solving with; problem-solving, the unknown, discomfort, passion, drive, focus and overall discipline".

Given our focus in *Deep Health*, we wanted to know, as a scientist, how she gathered and analyzed data today, including through artificial intelligence.

"Part of my job function at work is to gather and analyze data from production to assess the health of our process. Current methods for doing this involve the production staff manually entering data into an online database for the shop-floor. This data is then transferred to an analytics program where data trending can occur but is manually done by the subject matter experts. A feature of this data capturing is that the [subject matter experts] have selected parameters for their process, which are critical or key. We get alerted electronically if there is an abnormality in the data. This then prompts us to look at the data and make decisions on actions to be taken, whether it is to monitor the parameter or to stop and fix the issue."

Brittany's pursuit of helping others does have some connection to artificial intelligence. "For my direct function, we do not have much in the way of AI since we are using equipment to fit a process from the 1960s. However, the exciting future of my drug substance and the company is that we will be moving to a facility being built with full automation and AI. Online readings will be taken, and the AI will be able to adapt to the changes in the process within the setpoint parameters. All of our records will be electronic and will prompt each part of the process to confirm that the records of the step before are completed and approved."

Brittany's employer is not stopping there. "As preparation for this exciting change, the company has begun to build a team of AI educators that will help integrate all current employees into their new roles interacting with the AI in the new facility. It is an exciting time to be in both science and manufacturing."

The world of biochemical science/vaccines is changing as a result of AI, and Brittany's team will be leveraging the technology. "AI will assist with the ability to produce quality vaccines (or biologics) in an efficient manner and with reproducibility. One thing that needs to be considered in a manual process is the influence of the human component. You can have operator biases that aren't noticed but can impact batch to batch variability."

We turned our focus to boxing, asking Brittany whether she shared her training and workout data with her trainer, and if so, how it was used? "During COVID-19 we did an online spreadsheet of all my training, and sent videos of workouts. Adapting to the change in how we could train. We let up a bit on the food component to reduce stress on my body and anxiety levels were higher during this time. For the monitoring beforehand, the main emphasis was to reduce [body fat percentage] and weight simultaneously. We had to balance carefully as muscle mass would increase as I was lifting heavier, or boxing for power/strength.   We were also careful how much to monitor my data as you can become consumed with the data too and not allow yourself to feel out the signals your body is giving you".

For boxing athletes, various AI tools are now available, so we wanted to know what Brittany had experienced or researched. "BotBoxer is very interesting to me. The ability of the Bot to learn and react to your punches is amazing. When you see boxers train with it, there is a level of intensity that mimics a real fight. You need speed, agility, and quick reaction times. I have also seen reviews from top-level boxers where they say that variability in the intensity levels allows for you to really refine skills without needing a partner to train with you. There is also the ideal situation of the live data generation so you can see your progress in real-time."

Looking to the future, we asked Brittany how she saw the world of boxing changing as a result of AI. "I think in the world of boxing, and also other athletic worlds, we will see the athletes' abilities rise to levels that we haven't seen before. Training will be able to be better tailored to each athlete, and there will be better information for camps or coaching teams to understand the needs of their athlete to excel. I think that overall, boxers will be able to visualize their speed, force, etc. as they train, which will help to understand small manipulations that can be made to a movement to increase the effectiveness of the punch or movement. Of course, there is always the chance that too much data can consume you. There will be a fine line for how much data one athlete can utilize and still be effective in the mental part of the game. You don't want to always be waiting for the shots where you know you have the most force for a knock-out but live in the moment and react."

After speaking to Brittany, we identified an excellent opportunity to conduct a follow-up interview with her trainer to understand his view of technology's influence, including offerings like, **PIQ** and other wearable sensors for punch count, power level/force, retraction time, speed, etc.

Interview with a Boxing Trainer

Harold Rose, High-Performance Manager at High Definition Sports & Fitness, is Brittany's coach and trainer. He is a believer in AI-related tools like wearables, cameras, and fixed equipment. He uses several instruments, including high-speed cameras and video analysis apps. He is a big fan of wearable technology like heart rate monitors and ergometers that capture real-time data to quantify training improvement and effectiveness. His philosophy, like many of the best coaches and trainers, is what you measure, you improve. "High-speed cameras help with identifying and educating a client on movement efficiency. Heart rate monitors help with being an indicator or work and recovery. The resting heart rate is a great KPI [Key Performance Indicator] on how the body's recovering. With the corrective app I use, you're able to plug in assessment data, and it takes the expertise of the doctors who designed it and gives me an instant prescription that's more objective."

Harold also incorporates a cardio coach to test Vo2 max, another touchpoint for the body's ability to use oxygen and teach proper breathing. We asked him if consumers/non-elite athletes can benefit from these tools to improve their health and live longer, healthier.

"Absolutely, at the highest levels, elite athletes do simple things at a very high level, and they are amazing compensators. With movement quality, everyone can benefit from it. Understanding movement not being bad or good but more effective or less effective due to risk factors." He continued, "The heart is a great indicator to measure intensity because of its reflexive nature. When a person's resting heart rate is lower, it is a sign of a healthy heart. When we see fluctuations, it's a KPI that the workload needs to be altered. I think of it similar to when you go into a hospital or the doctor, and they check your vitals. This is a litmus test for your wellbeing. If they notice irregularities, then it's a clear sign you are not well and need prescriptive measures or to be monitored more closely. Using simple technology can help us all safely improve our health."

Stephanie Marcil, the skier and former member of the Canadian National Ski Team and AI enthusiast, believes using AI to improve athletic performance will be a game-changer. "When win or lose is a matter of milliseconds, every incremental improvement is significant. Current athletes have multiples coaches with different specialties. But in the future, they will only need one. AI is the ultimate coach because it will have all the insights and capabilities to do it all. It will know an athlete more than they know themselves and tell them when to rest and what to eat, create a personalized nutrition and physical training plans, monitor hydration status, nutrition status, heart rate, sleep, stress level and much more. Future athletes will look nothing like the ones we have now. AI will unlock our human potential and create the next level athletes of the future".

PrecisionWEAR, an advanced sports wearable, allows athletes to both optimize performance and reduce injuries. The garments advise the wearer of their unique reaction to training activities through stride imbalance, force, velocity, stress, and more totalling 21 factors, making them understandable.

Athletes benefit from support in decision-making about the level, duration of various training activities, and whether they lead to the wearer's objectives, including preventing injuries. Indeed, with advancing tech like 5G, artificial intelligence, cloud storage and more, wearable technology will only improve.

Makenzie Alger is a blogger with Aspire Ventures. In a 2017 post, she argued that those athletes with hardcore routines, and clean diets, generally live longer, have lower heart rates, and are usually happier. Can artificial intelligence help you at each stage of the workout - training, performing, and recovering? When considering your food intake in relation to fitness, artificial intelligence helps you at each step of the workout, including training, performing and recovering. Each stage requires energy, and AI can monitor the foods you eat and resulting glucose levels to sustain your energy. **KingFit** is one example that purports to "track glucose levels and provide the user with recommended eating plans based on the monitored results." By using personalized reminders and alerts, the app helps the user maintain a routine for their diets.

AI and Connected Fitness

Working from home, and with our neighbourhood gyms being closed or having limited access, doesn't mean we need to forgo our fitness regimens. With increased connectivity (4G and 5G), manufacturers of "smart" gym equipment will have the ability to take their equipment and programs to expansive and more immersive workouts.

"Connected Fitness," which includes the wearables and apps we have discussed in this book, is expanding into smart workout equipment that we can use in our homes. One such example is Apple Watch now connecting and pairing with compatible gym equipment, allowing you to track and record your workout.

Rob has his stationary bicycle mounted and connected to his **TACX** cycle trainer. With his laptop connected and mounted in front of him, he experiences cycling through the streets of London, Paris or the fictional world of Watopia. The system delivers an immersive and full workout complete with climbs, speed, cadence, and distance. His heart rate monitor syncs seamlessly with the program and is recorded for the duration of his workout.

As at-home workouts become more popular, numerous companies offer and promote interactive equipment and exercises. Fightcamp, Peloton, Mirror and Bowflex are just a few examples.

Fightcamp

Fightcamp offers those inclined to practice boxing an interactive training system. Launched in 2018, this home gym comes with a freestanding punching bag, gloves, quick wraps and access to on-demand instructional classes. Fightcamp is also adding other training activities (powered by motion recognition algorithms) to their program, including kicks, push-ups, and jump rope.

Peloton

The ever-ubiquitous and popular stationary bike has carved out its' own niche for those that want the ultimate at-home cycling experience and workout. To date, they have sold over 400,000 units. Peloton on-demand workout programs allow you to follow instructors and keep you motivated!

Mirror

Mirror is an interactive monitor that doubles as a mirror when not in use. Mirror offers a subscription service with on-demand fitness workouts. According to CEO Brynn Putnam, "We're vying to be the next screen in your life, not the next treadmill in your home. You have your phone for communication, your computer for information, your TV for entertainment and now the Mirror for experiences." Their subscription service gives access to pre-recorded workouts, including yoga, cardio fitness, Pilates and resistance training.

Bowflex

Bowflex has pivoted to the AI platform with its system called *Max Intelligence.* Their library of trainer-led videos and educational content offers programs based on how the user is feeling, how much time they have. They also measure your fitness level by using a 14-minute performance test.

With companies capitalizing on increased connectivity and AI platforms, working out and staying fit from home has never been as accessible, engaging or as immersive as today.

Endurance & Health

In sports, infinitely small measurements can mean the difference between winning and losing. A player's performance, working in teams, competitive factors, history, trends, and physiological factors play a role in informing organizational leaders, coaches, and players. AI is no longer a luxury, but a competitive advantage that only some are beginning to take advantage of and is becoming mandatory at elite levels.

Do Athletes Live Longer? *Labmate* says that team sports, with their inherent discipline and heightening of interaction, can support lifelong exercise.

Olympic athletes are considered amongst the world's best-trained performers in sports. Do they live longer than non-athletes? Well, the British Medical Journal tried to answer that question by tracking over 15,000 individuals who had competed since 1986 when the Olympics were resurrected. They compared survival rates 30 years from the Olympics they had participated in, with non-athletes of the same age from the same country.

Maybe not surprisingly, there was a difference. Firstly, the Olympians tended to live longer than non-Olympians but not in equal measure. There was a difference between endurance and power sport Olympic athletes. Endurance sports like marathon running, swimming and biathlon had longer life expectancy than those who took part in the shot put or weightlifting. 13% more endurance athletes were alive after 30 years, and only 5% more power athletes, according to an article by Luke Bradshaw, Sports Editor at Culture Trip.

So why was this the case? One view is presented by the American Medical Association in their 2001 study, which looked at the maximum amount of oxygen a body can take during exercise (VO2max). Sports like long-distance running require the athlete to work harder to move oxygen into the lungs, whereas sports like boxing and powerlifting do not have the same level of demands. When the study considered endurance athletes, it showed they had a 43% lower risk of dying at a given age, team athletes a 33% lower risk, and 10% for power sports. So, the AMA argued that the more your body has to work to obtain oxygen, the greater your chances of longevity.

In a 2015 paper published on PMC (PubMed Central) authors Srdjan Lemez, Assistant Professor at California State Polytechnic Institute and Joseph Baker, Professor and Head of the Lifespan Health and Performance Laboratory in the School of Kinesiology and Health Science, at York University, Canada. They argue that there is evidence to support the idea that moderate exercise for a lifetime is better than competitive level exercise for only a short period of your life.

One wearable device that aligns with endurance athletes is called *Humon*. This device measures the bodies' lactic acid threshold while attached to a working muscle like the leg. Oxygenated blood is measured by shining light into the skin, tracking changes in blood color. Such measurements offer a way to track endurance improvements.

Artificial intelligence provides a way to personalize the data collection for athletes, customized their performance plan to one body, and giving them the appropriate signals for exertion and endurance. Notably, resistance training can reduce muscle wasting and bone strengthening.

Movement Efficiency

Athletic performance is as much about flexibility and balance as any other factor. Analysing movement and obtaining the highest movement efficiency requires determining the least amount of energy spent for the highest degree of performance. Efficiency levels can be determined using artificial intelligence.

Wearables, like Atlas devices, monitor movement in a 3D space, comparing each exercise and the effect on the body. The need for expensive trainers and equipment is reduced for the average consumer when AI devices become available off the shelf.

Connexion comes equipped with a myriad of sensors on an AI-powered platform to host health applications. Connexion partnered with *Fusionetics* to offer a movement efficiency screening solution for automated health assessments, pinpointing which body parts are efficient and which ones are not.

Yoga

Yoga is recognized as one of the world's most popular fitness activities, with over 300 million regularly practicing, taking advantage of yoga's multiple benefits, including reducing anxiety and depression and thwarting the onset of such chronic diseases such as obesity and diabetes. US consumers spend over $15 billion annually on equipment and accessories, and in the current pandemic environment, those numbers are surging. Over $31 billion is spent annually on yoga clothing growing at a 6% compound annual growth rate, while equipment like yoga mats generate $13 billion.

The downward dog and tree pose activity have also found artificial intelligence in smartphone apps recording and analyzing yoga sessions and performing posture-recognition, especially for the at-home market. *Zenia,* a virtual yoga assistant, developed by an engineer, offers a personalized approach to each yoga student monitoring progress and providing performance feedback through algorithms of computer vision and neural networks. Recognizing at least 16 major joint movements and sharing effectively real-time feedback through 4 guided courses and over a dozen sequences varying in length and intensity. Zenia bases its assessments on the AI-powered analysis of thousands of asana images under professional yoga instructors' oversight.

The software does not record video or store images for privacy's sake. Like any digital coach, the software can serve as an effective intermediary between sessions with a professional yoga instructor where yogis can enjoy calming scents, clean and minimalist decoration, and spa-like atmosphere.

Another example is AI-powered *Yoganotch* which uses wearable 3D motion sensors to check your yoga form in real-time, providing customized feedback and classes with the aim of making the user a better poser. Yoga teachers can also leverage the power of AI through *MixPose,* which uses *PoseNet* pose estimation networks from

Jetson Nano for pose recognition of various yoga positions. Teachers and students remotely engage through Android TV or mobile phones using AI pose estimation algorithms to nudge students by capturing their skeletal outlines and sharing virtual feedback on their poses.

Hydration & Health

We rarely think about how much water we consume, yet it is one of the most critical aspects of health. Most of us are probably dehydrated and don't realise it. Dehydration signs include dark urine (urine should be pale yellow to clear), less frequent urination, fatigue, dizziness, confusion, and extreme thirst. The standard advice is to drink eight glasses of water per day (one glass is 8 ounces or 237 ml). This "one size fits all" recommendation does not work for everyone. Depending on your height, weight and activity level, some of us will require more or less.

The best way to determine your optimal level of water consumption is to calculate using this formula: Half your body weight in ounces. So, in Rob's case: 195 lbs/ 2 = 97.5 ounces or 2.88 L per day (without activity). Rob consumes up to 4 L per day, depending on his activity level and sweat rate. Rob tracks his fluid consumption using the "*My Water*" app. This simple app allows Rob to enter all his fluid consumption, including coffee, wine, smoothies, etc. The app will automatically update-so Rob knows precisely how much water he consumed.

Personalized hydration has been a focus of Gatorade, who developed the Gx platform. In this case, measuring sweat content, such as sodium and electrolytes, Gx offers a personalized drink formula, replenishing those 'sweated away' nutrients. Going further, smart caps on water bottles tracking fluid intake are part of Gatorade's innovation paradigm, promoting healthier hydration. Artificial intelligence helps athletes track fluid concentration levels on a personalized basis.

Fasting and Body Waste Controls and Flushing

Fasting can offer an excellent alternative for those who are plateauing in their weight. Fasting, as a process, is based on the glymphatic system in your body. The glymphatic system refers to a macroscopic waste clearance system that uses perivascular channels, created by astroglial cells, to promote the efficient purging of soluble proteins and metabolites from the central nervous system. Fasting enthusiasts argue that by restricting your intake of food for 13, 16, or 18 hours, the body consumes the available sugar then draws on the fat stored in your body, thus reducing body weight. We use this technique at least once a week, usually overnight, from 7 pm to 10 am with only a cup of black coffee in between.

Plateauing

When I (Brian) lost over 25 pounds during the first two years of my 'retirement,' I was exhilarated. I felt lighter. I could walk upstairs without losing my breath. Then I hit a plateau. I found I wasn't losing any more weight. Yes, I was working out and building muscle mass, which weighed more than fat. Still, according to my scale, I had too much body fat as a percentage of my overall weight. It certainly was frustrating seeing the same plus or minus five pounds every day on the scale despite trying different methods of exercise, calorie intake, and work-related activities (trying to reduce my number of minutes or hours sitting at the computer).

Now it does not mean I'm not fit. It merely means I needed to understand the nature of plateauing, and this is where tracking (yes, more data) comes in.

Tracking the type of calories you're consuming makes a big difference. There are significantly more calories in a 100-gram slice of pizza than in a 100-gram apple (280 versus 50). While Friday nights remain a pizza night tradition, I had lots of room the rest of the week to make better choices if I wanted to get my body fat down to an acceptable, non-athlete level of 17% (from 25%).

When you're exercising, the body uses up the sugars stored in your body first, then goes after the fat as an energy source. Similarly, when fasting (for me, it's 13-18 hours maximum), your body goes through the sugar stores, then burns the fat in your body until new food is introduced to provide energy.

Tracking is wonderful; however, my brain and stomach had a constant argument over whether I was truly hungry or not. My stomach, notwithstanding my need for more healthy calories, was sending signals to my brain that I was hungry for more dense calories like pizza.

This is where motivation kicks in. Reinforcing your goals, and the reason you are doing what you're doing has to overcome that biological sensation. Rob's recommendation for fasting made a huge difference for me.

Chapter 6

Your Microbiome

Humans are like mobile warm-blooded coral reefs, home to vast numbers of microbial systems that are rich in biodiversity – Dr. Robert Roundtree

Our bodies harbour up to 100 trillion distinct microbes, including viruses, fungi, bacteria and protozoa. Collectively these microbes are known as the microbiome. Our microbiome can affect our mood, weight, longevity and overall health. More importantly, when this complex ecosystem functions the way it should, it protects us from pathogens and is central to a healthy immune system. It is estimated that our gut microbiome modulates 70% of our immune system. The microbiome on its own is estimated to weigh as much as 5 pounds! Some considered the microbiome a living organism unto itself, and it is often referred to as your second brain. Microbial cells differ from human cells by their composition and structure, and they populate areas of our body, including skin, mouth, nose and eyes.

As in the case of DNA, microbiome analysis, enabled by faster, higher-capacity, and ever more sophisticated artificial intelligence technologies, will cost less to assess. New tools to analyze your microbiome are becoming available from firms like *Micron*.

Is our microbiome more critical than our DNA? It depends upon which scientist or researcher you speak to, but from our perspective, both are critical to understanding your unique qualities. Both are incredibly complex. According to The Human Genome Project, humans have between 20,000 and 25,000 genes. The microbiome encodes over 3 million genes that produce thousands of metabolites (as per Gut Microbiota for Health.com). In terms of genes, humans are more than 99% microbial! Fortunately, we have artificial intelligence to analyse trillions of bits of data in a reasonably short time (often minutes) detecting patterns undetectable by traditional human methods.

In the last few years, the microbiome has become much more prominent in food and nutrition. One of the primary functions of the microbiome is to help digest foods including dietary fibers. The by-product of this digestion is short-chain fatty acids (SCFA's). SCFA's play a key role in disease and health.

The microbiome also helps with the absorption of many dietary minerals like calcium and magnesium and also synthesizes specific essential amino acids and vitamins (e.g. Vitamin B9 and Vitamin K). Our microbiome varies individual to individual and can be affected by environment, diet, genetics and gender. It is severely impacted by toxins, medications, stress, age and antibiotic use. When this delicate ecosystem is not functioning the way it should, we are more susceptible to infection and chronic disease.

Probiotics and Prebiotics are often touted as a way to help balance the gut flora and help to "heal" our guts after trauma such as long-term antibiotic use. But how do we know the optimal probiotic? How much prebiotic fiber should we consume?

A research team from the University of New South Wales in Australia is commercializing a new indigestible capsule that will analyze your gastrointestinal gases when swallowed. As the capsule moves through your gut, it measures the various gases produced by your microbiome and transmits this data to your smartphone. This will be valuable for studies on food digestion, normal gut function and microbiome studies.

Several AI-powered microbiome home tests exist today. *Viome* offers a 'Gut Intelligence' Test. According to *Viome*, this will provide you with "comprehensive health insights about your gut microbiome that empower you to make the best lifestyle and nutrition choices." *Viome* is a simple at-home stool test and questionnaire. When results are available, *Viome* will send you a complete microbiome health analysis, including a personalized 90-day nutrition plan and supplement recommendations. This information can be viewed on the smartphone app, and it syncs with Apple Health. *Viome* recommendations are designed to encourage foods compatible with your metabolism, help the user increase microbial species generally associated with wellness, and reduce those related to poor health. *Viome* also seeks to help the user determine the ideal ratio of fats, carbs and proteins for their diet.

IBM and the University of California San Diego completed a study seeking to understand whether the human microbiome (and which location) was a useful indicator of age. It turns out that the skin microbiome was the most accurate predictor within a few years of actual age. Notably, microbes in the gut and oral area in younger subjects were more abundant than in older subjects suggesting the loss of key microbes over a lifetime. Using machine learning, IBM and UCSD illustrated that indicators of age (both accurate and generalizable) could be established.

Dr. Eric Topol, an American cardiologist, scientist, author, and founder and Director of the Scripps Research Translational Institute, wrote an article in 2019 in the New York Times about an interesting experience. Topol participated in a two-week experiment, during which he tracked all the food, beverage and medication he consumed, monitored his blood glucose and the amount he slept and exercised.

Topol participated in this study with a thousand others to have their data collected and analysed by artificial intelligence to create a personalized diet to perhaps help them live a longer, healthier life. It became even clearer to Topol, that no one diet that was optimal for all people.

People are unique and have different physiologies. They react differently to foods, environmental impacts, and exercise.
What Topol's experience proved was that universal, one size fits all diets do not work, and we are naïve to think so. Each of us is remarkably diverse and unique when it comes to our microbiome, metabolism, and environment. An optimal diet also needs to be varied and individualized for each of us.

We are starting to see the emergence of companies marketing nutrigenomics. Nutrigenomics is the study of the interaction of nutrition and genes, concerning the prevention or treatment of disease with the potential to influence our approach to diet and exercise.

The complexity of customizing a personalized diet can only be tackled by Artificial Intelligence. AI is required to analyse billions of bytes of data about each person. This would include your DNA makeup and your unique microbiome, medical history, family history, lifestyle, current health status, etc.

Chapter 7

The Brain & Sleep

Reviewing the history of the development of artificial intelligence clearly reveals that brain science has resulted in breakthroughs in AI.
– Jingtao Fana, Lu Fang, Jiamin Wua, Yuchen Guoa, Qionghai Daia

As our brains age, mental acuity often declines and is one of the most feared consequences of growing old. We asked ourselves, 'What if we can be more effective at training our brains to stay fit and slow cognitive decline'? People are starting to look for answers and are seeing more and more AI-powered options on the market.

We know that memory, attention span, thinking activities, sensory acuity, and visual exercises are essential to your brain's long-term health. Specific AI-powered applications like *NeuroTracker* offer cognitive training for scientific, academic, athletic, and medical purposes, testing the user for all the preceding capabilities. Virtual and augmented reality training solutions also engage the brain in stimulating focus and attention and decision-making. AI is the engine for many of these solutions, monitoring brain patterns by location and signal strength. The objective of programs like *NeuroTracker* is to boost brainwave activity, improve cognitive functions, and increase neuroplasticity (becoming more adaptive).

84

Muse is a brain-sensing headband with seven electroencephalography (EEG) sensors. Created to help the user manage stress, Muse provides insights into what's happening in your brain sending, the sensor data via Bluetooth to your smartphone or laptop for audio or text messages. Having tried this device on numerous occasions, one does achieve a sense of serenity through combined meditation and calming music. The clarity in the brain through solutions like Muse can support your cognitive health and your understanding of how your brain patterns work.

Nathan Copeland, quadriplegic and research participant at the University of Pittsburgh, loves his implants. The Utah Array brain-computer interface embedded in his head allows Nathan, a victim of a car accident that left him without movement in either arms or legs, to play video games like Sonic Hedgehog 2, his favorite activity. Nathan, the only human known to have a somatosensory cortex (signals for the sense of touch) implant, considers himself lucky to have these abilities. Other groups are exploring the brain-computer interface like *Neuralink*, Elon Musk's new venture.

Neuralink is developing a brain interface device with an implantable array of 3,000 flexible, ultra-thin electrodes to augment brain function and stimulate nerve cells. The Neuralink chip, called N1, is smaller in size than a coin and incorporates 1,024 electrodes no wider than a human hair. Neuralink will be powered by an external battery that looks like an old hearing aid battery placed behind the ear. The initial focus of the chip is the treatment of quadriplegic patients with c1-c4 spinal injury.

The ultra-high bandwidth interface seeks to restore limb function, eyesight and hearing in its way. In the case of hearing, Neuralink is expected to "extend the range of hearing beyond normal frequencies and amplitudes", according to Elon Musk, even providing access to streaming music directly from the chip connecting wirelessly to your smartphone or other device. Musk predicts the implantable chip offers future *Deep Health* type capabilities, including communicating without words, detecting epileptic attacks, and restore memories for those who have Alzheimer's. Connecting with artificial intelligence will ultimately augment the data processing capability of the Neuralink interface.

As published in the journal Nature Communications, a team funded by Facebook Reality Labs developed a brain-computer interface program that "accurately decodes dialogue—words and phrases both heard and spoken by the person wearing the device—from brain signals in real-time." By directly decoding speech originating from brain signals from two different parts of the brain, provides context and an increase in decoding accuracy. Augmented reality glasses will externally listen to brain signals using infrared light and offer the ability to be controlled without speaking aloud.

As algorithms improve, and computer processing speeds increase, overlaying increased accuracy of artificial intelligence capabilities through context, humans, particularly those in need, will benefit in so many ways. Whether it's those who have lost the ability to speak due to stroke or other injury, or communication in new and undiscovered situations, context is an important advance in the field of AI, and the brain is at the heart of the research.

Artificial Intelligence, the Brain & Speech Health

In 2019, I attended my daughter's convocation ceremony at Dalhousie University in Halifax, Nova Scotia, Canada. The institution has been around since 1818 and graduates thousands of bright students every year. The ceremony I attended was for Health Science related graduates - specialties like Kinesiology, Health Administration, Audiology, and my daughter's focus - Speech-Language Pathology or SLP. SLP methodology, centered around communication disorders resulting from strokes, or childhood development, for example, is critical to the ability of those so affected.

At the post-convocation reception, the SLP Acting Department Head made the statement that really resonated with me. "Twenty years ago, SLP's practice was very different from today, and twenty years from now, it will be very different again". It's not just consumers who need to make use of AI. Healthcare practitioners also need to leverage AI for patient health. So, let's cast our minds forward twenty years.

Let's assume that medical science has not completely solved the causes of speech disorders. As AI progresses, it is not too hard to believe that AI will be able to analyze, interpret, and replicate the thought patterns of an individual, and then communicate them outwardly in any language chosen? And that could be only one possible future.

As a firm believer in the advantage of balanced human and AI capabilities operating together, I predict the SLP practitioner would be able to guide the client/patient on an emotional/human journey, augmented by even greater tools. SLP's today go well beyond a process when they empathize, listen, and share the struggles of those they interact with. Being human, that won't likely change even 20

87

years in the future. So, combining AI with human SLP expertise, the future is bright for those in need.

The Future of SLP and Artificial Intelligence

Certain components of artificial intelligence have great potential in improving overall teletherapy effectiveness. Examples of the role of AI in remote delivery of health care existing today include the use of tele-assessment, tele-diagnosis, tele-interactions and tele-monitoring. Below, we will explore three examples of these AI technologies.

Consider recording tele-sessions. History-taking is often a time-consuming challenge for SLP's. Instead, filing a recorded session (with the assumption of compliant security capabilities and privacy controls) is a significant benefit. Running that recording through an AI algorithm could provide additional insights. Through speech to text technology, sentiment analysis software (using natural language processing) could be deployed to identify the speaker's mood more accurately during a session. Session content could be analysed for the frequency of word use.

The next example is emotion recognition. By studying and analysing patients' facial reactions during a teletherapy session, specific AI-powered software can recognize human emotions based on facial cues or physiological responses. *Affectiva* is one such emotion measurement technology company that grew out of MIT's Media Lab, enabling software applications to use a webcam to track a user's smirks, smiles, frowns and furrows, thus measuring the user's levels of surprise, amusement or confusion. *Affectiva*, which has analyzed over 9 million faces to date, is sensorless, permitting heart rate to be measured by tracking facial color changes every time the heart beats. Armed with this type of information, the SLP would be better able to assess the patient's reactions to the teletherapy activities without actually being there. The SLP has overriding decision-making on what information is used in the assessment. The privacy issue must be addressed; however, emotion recognition software could be assistive in the assessment process.

Ethical, privacy and social considerations must be taken into account when assessing whether artificial intelligence solutions should be embedded in teletherapy. In that vein, we provide several resources below to review.

What about automated conversations? Conversations in the online realm can have human-guided, patient-guided, and computer-guided approaches. Teletherapy is dependent upon phone and computer-based technology and focuses on the practitioner-client interaction. But what about when the practitioner is not available? Are there applications for an ai-powered surrogate? Apps like reminders and motivational messages, e.g., for medication, nutrition, and exercises interim to the next practitioner session, condition checks, providing articles or other information specific to the client, setting up meetings and taking notes during those meetings (like Zoom's AI functions) between intermediaries, and service agencies are all capabilities within today's AI world. According to the authors of the Role of Artificial Intelligence within the Telehealth Domain - Official 2019 Yearbook Contribution by the members of IMIA Telehealth Working Group, "AI can make history taking easier by providing prompts to the process and clues to the diagnosis, and also asking the right next set of questions based on the answer saving the clinician time".

Could some of these capabilities be monitored by a parent interim to the next teletherapy session, increasing the therapy frequency and, in some instances, earnestly hoping for an improvement in the client or patient at a faster pace? As AI advances, verbal interactions between client and a conversational AI avatar with access to a client's medical and session history, may also advance to permit a practitioner to increase their client load, address the shortage of SLP's, while offering unique services to a growing population of clients.

While the future remains uncertain, tele-therapists who need to work remotely, in an environment where demand for services is growing, may benefit from the incredible potential of artificial intelligence.

Sleep and AI

Does it matter whether you're an early bird or a night owl in terms of your longevity? And what does that have to do with artificial intelligence? According to Kristen L. Knutson & Malcolm von Schantz in their paper entitled "Associations between chronotype, morbidity and mortality in the UK Biobank cohort," it does matter. Those who wake up earlier in the morning have a greater chance of living longer (both Rob and I live by the earliest opening times at Starbucks).

Chronotype refers to your waking time preference. For those who wake later in the morning, previous studies have shown a greater instance of metabolic dysfunction and cardiovascular disease (CVD). The above-noted study by Knutson and von Schantz, which took place in the UK over the period 2010 – 2017, included over 500,000 citizens aged 37-73. The study concluded that their "Mortality risk in evening types may be due to behavioural, psychological and physiological risk factors, many of which may be attributable to chronic misalignment between internal physiological timing and externally imposed timing of work and social activities."

What were some of the health challenge differences between early birds and night owls? The latter are 30 percent more likely to have diabetes and twice as likely to have a psychological disorder, along with higher rates of respiratory and gastrointestinal diseases. All is not lost for night owls, however. Gradual changes in sleep patterns, including earlier bedtime, can improve your chances of better health. According to Dr. Paul Kasenene, several studies illustrate a 50% increase in obesity for those experiencing less than 6 hours of sleep per night by altering the hormones involved in glucose metabolism and increasing appetite.

So, where does AI come in? The timelier the diagnosis of sleep disorders or issues with artificial intelligence solutions (i.e. enhanced polysomnograms tests), the faster treatment can be administered. AI can analyse brain waves, blood oxygen levels, REM vs deep sleep, heart rate, sleep duration, eye and leg movements, and more providing sleep professionals a more transparent, more accelerated insight of sleep performance.

Having a wearable that monitors your sleep cycles and wakes during a period of light sleep could improve your overall health by ensuring you are not woken during a REM or deep sleep cycle during which time you are getting the optimal health benefits. Smart Sleep Alarms, which come in free and paid apps, can improve your sleeping. Free apps include *Sleep as Android* for Android users and *Sleep Cycle* for iOS users. Apps that come with a smartwatch may be most accurate and convenient as they monitor your nighttime movement.

Trends in Cognitive Science reported in 2018 that REM (Rapid Eye Movement) and Non-REM sleep are very different. Non-REM sleep is more linear in the sense that the brain replays acquired memories equentially. On the other hand, REM sleep involves more disparate memories randomly displayed in your mind during sleep. From an AI perspective, REM sleep is analogous to deep learning (see definitions in the appendices) where novel insights are discovered through repetition and pattern exploration. As our brains fluctuate between the two states, they are learning and building associations from both sequential and random memories.

I use the Samsung Active Watch 2 daily. It provides me with an in-depth analysis of my sleep patterns. Rob's Apple Watch 4 sleep data is captured 24/7 and uploaded to the Apple Health app. Every morning I review my sleep stats logged by my Samsung smartwatch. It shows me four key measurements. How much of my total sleep time was light sleep, REM sleep, deep sleep, and awake time? Then it gives me a sleep efficiency rating.

So, monitoring your sleep patterns daily can provide insights into what activities lead to better sleep, i.e. when you eat, what you eat, the impact of blue light, how long you're on electronics, and more. Lack of sleep has shown to increase the risk of cancer, heart disease, obesity, high blood pressure, compromised immunity and even premature death.

Most people sleep for approximately a third of their lives. We tend to focus on the quantity of sleep and often overlook the importance of the quality of sleep. In the U.S. about 35% of the population does not get enough sleep. In today's digital, always-on lifestyle, people use their electronics to fall asleep, but that is often a fateful decision, as it negatively impacts their sleep.

The American Sleep Association recently concluded that sleep disorders exist for 50 to 70 million US adults, including insomnia, sleep apnea, narcolepsy, and circadian rhythm disorders. Unemployed citizens have the highest likelihood of sleep disorder or negative impact, followed by those who report being unable to work. Education level also appeared to have an impact according to the study with a college degree or higher, having better sleep experience and duration. Finally, married people reported healthier sleep duration than never married, divorced, widowed or separated individuals. According to the HR firm, RAND, the financial impact of sleep-deprived employees is as high as $411 billion. In the UK, it translates into 207,000 working days a year from absenteeism, decreased productivity, and even mortality.

Beyond the Apple Watch and Samsung Active Watch Rob and I use, there are other AI-powered apps for sleep monitoring. For example, *Symple Symptom Tracker* is a free healthy lifestyle app that tracks how you feel, sleep, and eat to monitor those aspects of your health. Like most apps, it is simple to use, and by entering a few data points about how you feel and then share at your next doctors' appointment.

Sleep Cycle is a smart alarm clock that tracks your sleep patterns and designed to wake you during your lightest sleep cycle without a conventional alarm clock. As explained on their website, "Waking up during light sleep feels like waking up naturally." *Sonic Sleep* uses your mobile's microphone to analyse background noise then leverage an AI algorithm to filter out the right noises. *Sleep.ai* detects afflictions like snoring, teeth grinding, and sleep apnea through sound analysis. *SleepScore* monitors the users breathing rate and movement via a mobile speaker and microphone, then processes the data and compares to their database, providing insights into the user's sleep patterns.

Dreem is wearable headband technology. It utilizes machine learning at home to monitor your brain's activity, body movement and heart rate, emitting calming sounds for sleep, smart alarms and recommendations for breathing exercises. Finally, the *HEKA AI* mattress collecting data as you sleep through pressure distribution analysis, while in real-time adjusting the mattress for optimum sleep.

Outside of personal data collection, sleep centers offer a different data source for comparison purposes for artificial intelligence. Sleep clinics worldwide collect massive amounts of data from patients that feed machine learning and AI algorithms to make progress in our understanding and treatment of sleep care, personalization, predictions, and diagnoses.

Once you gain insights into your sleep patterns through AI-powered solutions, insights discovered can be shared with healthcare providers to assess patients' sleep patterns and disorders. Healthcare providers will be able to assess snoring pattern, daytime sleepiness or fatigue, then educate patients and share best practice sleep habits. In the business world, HR teams can share tips with their employees and appropriate work scheduling for sufficient sleep duration.

Chapter 8

Personal Journeys

"Do something today that your future self will thank you for" – Sean Patrick Flannery

Information is great, but what's the tipping point to make you act? For me, it was being overwhelmed with so much conflicting information. Experts were offering advice, contradicted by other experts or new studies. What to eat, the best exercises, new gadgets, the right mental health activities, always changing, and most of it was not personalized for my unique physiology. It was all too much, and as you will see in section 2 of this book, the genesis for the ***Deep Health*** concept.

The second motivating factor for me was my escalating dislike of traditional pharmaceutical medications. I reasoned that if I could address the root causes of my ailments, I could reverse and possibly cure them rather than mask the symptoms. I learned that tweaking my diet, introducing new exercises, reducing weight, and taking a health supplement and a myriad of other non-medication choices, my health started to improve beyond medications.

Today I'm more fit than I was at 30, partly due to better food choices (sadly, french fries were my main food staple back then). From my youthful years up to 2016, I was slowly increasing medication to combat symptoms from a laundry list of physical ailments, including type-2 diabetes, high cholesterol and triglycerides, high blood pressure, excess weight, shortness of breath, and a constant feeling of anxiousness.

The worst experience and significant turning point for me was something I called 'brain fire.' Brain fire is best described as a severe, overwhelming burning sensation that was utterly incapacitating. I later learned this is caused by chronic inflammation. According to The Conversation, a medical periodical, "repeated stress is a major trigger for persistent inflammation in the body. Chronic inflammation can lead to a range of health problems, including diabetes and heart disease. The brain is normally protected from circulating molecules by a blood-brain barrier. But under repeated stress, this barrier becomes leaky and circulating inflammatory proteins can get into the brain."

I vividly remember the night in a hotel in New Jersey when I experienced my worst' brain fire' episode. It was such an overpowering sensation. I travelled extensively (planes, trains, automobiles...you know the story), eating only processed hotel and restaurant foods full of sugars, carbs and salt, putting in long hours and scheduling back-to-back meetings. Sound familiar to any of our busy readers?

Brain fire felt like every part of my brain was overheating, and I could not think straight. For me, sleep deprivation, poor food choices, stress and obesity all led to the inflammation coursing throughout my body but especially my brain. Yet, I didn't understand all those connections at the time.

Brain fire led to cognitive challenges (diminishing performance by my prefrontal cortex or the thinking part of your brain) and elevated fight or flight reactions (powered by the amygdala section of your brain). My sleep suffered, and I continued to make more bad food choices, not a great combination when you're trying to work.

My health spiralled out of control (to which my family can attest), leading to the defining moment of my life when my doctor told me that I had to leave work for the sake of my health. I was only 52 years old. I was a successful executive in a top 10 North American bank. I ran an operations team of over 150 people in Canada, the US and indirectly in India. I was on a plane almost every week. My teams' (of whom I was so proud) were successfully fighting financial fraud worldwide. Yet I was being told I had to leave work. Within three short years of starting the role, I developed type 2 diabetes, high blood pressure, high cholesterol levels, and immeasurable stress with visible signs of declining physical and mental health. It was at that moment I had to make a choice. Continue pushing myself to an early grave or live in a whole new way.

Restarting My Life

The process I went through was gruelling. Initially, it felt like a boot camp where everything was uncomfortable. Shortly after leaving the corporate world, I slept for the better part of a month with only small periods of waking time as my body tried to reset itself. My recovery regimen began with a walk half-way down the block. It was all I could manage. Stairs were a nightmare carrying extra weight, and a weak circulatory system to the top. Shortness of breath, anxiety, and weakness in my legs often meant I could go no further. I returned from my neighborhood walk to my home only to go back to sleep.

Nutrition Changes – Slow and (Sometimes) Easy

For me, change had to be slow and progressive. I couldn't make all the changes at once. Diet soda was the first to go. A half-litre a day was the norm. By the way, switching to diet soda did nothing positive for my blood glucose level either. So, I turned to soda water (the colder, the better), and I didn't look back.

Carbs were next. I ate potatoes, in some form, at every meal. Hash browns in the morning, potato chips at lunch and French fries for dinner. I told myself that as long as there was something green on the plate, I was okay. Then I found out about simple versus complex sugars (thanks Rob!). Potatoes turn into simple sugars, which increase your blood glucose level more than almost any food type. I found it difficult to go 'cold turkey', so I reduced it to once a day. When my blood glucose still did not go down to a level I was happy with the potatoes went away.

If you're a carbs person, the following will be unhappy because the next to go was grains. I found that I would get stomach upset when I ate bread products, and in the past, I had just gotten used to it. Especially since I didn't know which vice was causing it. I started substituting meat slices for bread in my breakfast. It tasted great, and I soon forgot about adding a piece of toast with my breakfast. The same went for cereals. They are made from grains and usually augmented with a myriad of other additives and simple sugars. I used to love club sandwiches. You know the ones with layers. Three pieces of toast and the rest of the 'fixins'. Gone. Again, these choices were meant for one person, me.

There's more. Next to go was popcorn and corn. Corn is wonderful tasting (in fact, as kids we used to, wait for it, drink corn syrup!) and I could eat mountains of it. But corn turns into simple sugars in a big way. Your body doesn't need or want those simple sugars. They merely turn into fat. Popcorn for me was a large, butter-covered bag for every movie (how did I ever make it this far?). When I read the calorie content of a large bag of buttered popcorn (think 1500 calories plus or minus), I realized I didn't want three-quarters of my daily caloric intake in popcorn! Not to mention the salt!

Salt was next. Sometimes referred to those in my circle as 'white death', salt was a staple in my diet since I was a kid. We put salt on everything, even if it was already salted. Table salt's properties, unlike that of say iodized sea salt, contribute to several ailments.

Oh yes, the fun continues. Beer. I used to love a cold beer with friends on a patio in the middle of summer. So, refreshing. But something happened when grains became so apparent in my diet. I started feeling incredibly full from half of a beer. I could not finish a pint. Maybe my age was a factor, but I could not get past the full feeling, so I stopped drinking beer (fortunately appropriate portions of red wine is healthier and does not have the same effect).

Diet soda, potatoes, bread, corn, beer. All gone from my diet in the span of a year. I'm not saying it was easy; in fact, it was hard. The thought that kept going through my mind was, if I don't do something different, I'm going to be on these meds, and maybe more, for the rest of my life. I have a choice. Why not take the road that addresses the root causes, rather than the one that masks and fights the resulting problems?

I have a running game with my general practitioner. I arrive at her office and try to show off how fit I am. How much weight I've lost. How my blood glucose level is being controlled by my diet and fitness rather than the meds. I show her the stats I've gathered from my weigh scale, smartwatch, and smartphone. Her typical response is, "that's great, Brian; however, we still need to get to such an such a stage before eliminating your medication." Of course, I'm furious given all the work I've done, but I must accept her view as one of my healthcare advisors. So, I continue, striving to be meds free…for as long as I can.

Fitness Changes – One Step at a Time

Over the months following my retirement, the distance I could travel slowly extended to a few blocks, then a few kilometres. Every step was incremental. Five minutes on an exercise machine at my local gym slowly over a year turned into thirty. For me, the elliptical machine was a lifesaver (or more appropriately knee saver) after years of running half marathons. I found there was very little pressure on my knee joints and that I could, over time, improve the surrounding muscle, and combined with extensive walking, return to the road surfaces.

Weight training was another part of my recovery process. I found that over years of neglect, my muscles had atrophied to a certain extent. I found my back ached from lack of core body/abdomen strength, while my knees complained from the additional 30 pounds that I lugged around. Opening jars had become more of a 'my son' function. Hauling lumber around at the cottage required a few more trips. So, slowly increasing weights and working different body parts became part of my daily exercise regimen and allowed me to see progress without overdoing it. By the time a few months had passed, I was up to 30 minutes of weight training a session.

Seeing the changes in my body gave me a mental boost, reaffirming the choices I made and feeling better about myself and every activity I took part in. With the advent of the pandemic society we're in today, I, like many others, set up my home gym. Now I can maintain my fitness routine while listening to my favourite playlist and tracking my trends and progress.

Staying Healthy

This chapter is about motivation, and I've shared how I want to be medication-free for as long as possible. That and trying to solve for being overwhelmed with data is another. The final motivation for me is a story I experienced several years ago.

The mother of a relative of mine was being moved into a long-term care home. I offered to help move some furniture in, as this home permitted some personal items, including dressers and televisions. From the moment I stepped through the doors of the home, I smelled it. Urine. Everywhere. Now maybe being there for the first time, I was super sensitive to the smell. It overwhelmed me and remains with me to this day whenever I think about nursing or long-term care homes. I'm not suggesting all long-term care residences smell like this. They are desperately needed to deliver long term care to our elderly citizens. However, the impact of this olfactory experience leads me to my third motivation.

To stay as healthy as possible so that I can remain in my own home to a ripe old age. Many people have shared they have the same goal. I don't know if that's in the cards for me, but I am doing everything I can to achieve that goal. In three years, I have lost 30 pounds (13.6 kg), reduced my waist by 6 inches (15 cm), gained significantly more muscle mass, and reduced my overall body fat. It was a great sense of accomplishment when I minimized my Type 2 diabetes and got my blood pressure and cholesterol challenges under control. With each passing month, I realized that I was recovering, and the 'brain fire' had gone away and that there was hope.

Linking Health to AI

During my recovery period, I was in a position with enough energy to go after my business and career goals in a balanced way. I thought in a very preliminary way about what I wanted to do next. I couldn't decide so, and I developed a list of what I didn't want to do. That was much easier. After eliminating those tasks or roles, I started to envision what I could be. I couldn't say it would be for the rest of my life, but at least for the next year. I started to research technology, roles, trends, etc. since I had always been a liaison between business groups and IT teams and enjoyed it immensely. It made sense to me to pursue a technology specialty to support business leaders and those who wanted to benefit from technology.

I also decided that the technology needed to be sufficiently robust and trending. I chose the field of artificial intelligence, which in 2017 had just started to take-off. Once that choice was made, the next decision involved selecting and attending the best school on the planet for AI. Massachusetts Institute of Technology (MIT) was a wise choice because after I finished the 'AI Implications for Business Strategy' program, the phone started ringing. Those who had heard about AI but didn't know how to pursue it started contacting me for assistance, including the fitness and health fields.

From there, I realized I could reach a larger audience by writing a book. I made a conscious choice to do it myself, so I learned every skill I needed from, believe it or not, YouTube. Free advice from the planet. Since then, I have self-published three books on artificial intelligence, one an Amazon Bestseller, and this is my fourth. I work with large corporations, innovators, and AI enthusiasts - all extremely fulfilling pursuits.

You may want to follow my lead in choosing your path to eliminate all the things you don't want to do. If you've already selected a smaller group of passions, research them to a significant degree, including doing a "day-in-the-life" to see if the role is what you thought it would be. Also, the jobs of the future have yet to be created. Look at trends to see where technology, like AI, is moving tasks into automated hands, and where things like creativity, judgment, innovation, and instinct play an ongoing role for humans.

I feel that my work now has meaning. Today, my books have reached business leaders in 12 countries, including India, Brazil and Japan and I take great pride in knowing that I'm helping leaders find their way. The same applies to coaches who are beginning to see the benefits of artificial intelligence-powered tools to support coaching goals. I get to work with a whole new universe of AI enthusiasts in fields like healthcare, accounting, financial services, fitness, manufacturing and many more, helping them see the road ahead. Yet, I could not have done it all alone. Some wonderful people influenced my journey. They are my gurus.

Motivational Gurus

When Rob and I met in a Starbucks coffee shop many years ago, I had no idea the world that would open to me. Rob is a fountain of knowledge, and his high energy in sharing his thoughts and ideas makes you recoil sometimes. While I listened, I realized that I could only remember a few of the tidbits that Rob shared. Rob's knowledge and nutrition insights prompted me to review what I was doing on a daily basis (he kept bringing up the subject!), and the transformation for me was the journey I described above. No more diet soda, potatoes (except ironically sweet potatoes), corn, beer, bread products, milk chocolate, the list goes on. Rob inspired me to change my diet and continues today to be my source of nutrition knowledge and inspiration.

How about you? Do you have a health guru, mentor, or sage who can regularly share tidbits of insights with you? Rob never pressured me to change. He just offered up the benefits of each choice. As I write this, I sit here nibbling pistachio nuts. Rob recommended that I read a book from one of his favourite writers, Dr. David Perlmutter, who tells me they're good for my 'gut buddies' or microbiome. All of that would have been gobbledygook to me four years ago.

Dr. David Perlmutter is a Board-Certified Neurologist and five-time best-selling author. He is a voice of reason for a balanced view of the body, mind and health. In his 2020 book, *"Brain Wash"* written with his son Austin Perlmutter, David reminds us to be cautious of the amount of screen time we have each day (as we're writing this book, we have to laugh and laugh sigh!). The lesson is a valuable one, especially before you sleep. Not just minimizing your exposure to blue light but over-engaging your brain in news stories or anxiety-causing emails.

Robust *Deep Health* apps need to support you by alerting you of your screen time (synced to all your devices). Also, it should communicate with you via voice to lessen the strain on your eyes. Put the device on "text to voice" and let it talk to you, providing things like your daily briefing or when you're active in something much like the Samsung watch does today when you're working out.

Rob is an inspiration, and a prime source of daily motivation to be better than I was. He has been through his battles with cancer and weight gain and came out on the other side. I determined I should be able to do the same. Many of us may not have someone to inspire us. What if your smartwatch or other wearables can be your virtual "health coach" or inspiration? Both Rob and I often rely on our smartwatches to keep us on track and motivated during those times when we get off track.

Find your motivational gurus, leverage the power of artificial intelligence to get to know yourself better, and take the first steps to, as we began this chapter, "do something today that your future self will thank you for."

Chapter 9

Your Immunity

COVID-19 will "forever change the health and wellness sector" from a business point of view, as more people seek to cut through the nutrition clutter and have a trusted voice of authority" - Jason Brown, Founder and CEO of Persona Nutrition

The top global story of 2020 was undoubtedly the coronavirus pandemic. It impacted millions of people and killed hundreds of thousands worldwide. The long-term impact has yet to be realized. However, a few things are certain. People will take a harder look at their surroundings, proximity to others, and their health and fitness level to fight future viruses.

In Canada, over 80% of the recorded deaths due to COVID-19 occurred in long-term care and nursing homes where elderly individuals, especially those already compromised by other illnesses, were devastated. Citizens of countries where the coronavirus ravaged have become increasingly aware of their health and wellness.

During the COVID-19 lockdown in 2020, many people found it challenging to maintain their health. They gained weight (the COVID 15) and lost muscle strength due to not being able to go to the gym and sitting for long periods, whether working from home on virtual meetings or watching cable or social media.

Some took a different approach, creating home gyms. Home gym equipment sales skyrocketed. People looked for ways to "physical distance" while they ran, cycled or took on other kinds of activity. Bicycle sales soared. People that weren't running before used their previous office commute time for activities like running. Fitness trackers also became more popular as consumers looked to understand their fitness levels for a variety of activities (or non-activity in the case of sleep).

AI & Immunity

So, what critical contributors to your immunity are under your control, and how can AI help you? What if the companies you consumed goods from could help with navigating those nutritional science waters? Can personalized nutrition impact your immunity?

When consumers began to realize the impact of COVID-19, many who had spent little time thinking about their food choices started reading books, articles, and any other material to learn more about how food and lifestyle can impact immunity. Others began to realize that universal nutrition advice did not necessarily apply to them personally, given their unique physiology. The bottom line, staying healthy, reduced the risk of the coronavirus's most dangerous impacts, and nutrition could play a role in that effort.

According to Nutrition Insight, an online health periodical, one outcome of the COVID-19 virus was a "rapid personalization of sports nutrition as gyms around the world are increasingly shut, and sporting gatherings are banned." The world changed for many months, and local gym closures forced individuals to find alternatives. They said,

"...a study from Cell Science Systems stated that blood tests could reveal micronutrient and antioxidant deficiencies and allow a personalized way to bolster immunity and protect the body's cells."

Combine those two new dynamics with the telehealth phenomenon where consumers were increasingly meeting with doctors, clinicians, and advisors over the phone, or web meeting, and, despite privacy concerns, they were sharing data about their activity and nutrition because of their concern for the potential impact of the virus.

Increase use of online nutrition assessments translated into more personalized nutrition recommendations at companies like *Persona Nutrition*, a personalized nutrition service owned by Nestle Health Science. Further, some consumers have begun looking at nutritional supplements to augment their food choices to improve their immunity. A 2019 Oregon State study, published in the journal Nutrients, suggested that supplementation could be used for fighting COVID-19 as part of an overall public health recommendation. We mentioned *Supp.ai* as a solution to identify the interaction of nutritional supplements and medication. *Persona Nutrition* also cross-references medications with supplements before permitting customers to place their online orders.

Food choices also affect the trillions of microbes residing in your body. You are in effect, feeding them when you eat. The choices you make determine whether your 'gut buddies', as Dr. Stephen Gundry calls them, are well-nourished. The microbiome is key to a properly functioning immune system; it is critical to keep it well-nourished.

Exercise and Immunity

Globally, citizens of countries with high coronavirus infection rates have been social distancing in public indoor and outdoor settings. Runners who don't cohabitate are distancing or running solo. Former gym rats are working out at home. Many have adapted to their new environment and are still working out and remaining fit. But is there a belief that a continued regimen provides benefit in terms of immunity?

What are some of the benefits of being physically active in terms of immunity? Often physically active people may be less likely to infect others, have less severe symptoms, and reduced recovery times, according to the department of immunobiology at the University of Arizona, Tucson.

The pandemic turned our world upside down. Working in isolation has changed our routine, including the unintended consequence of exercising less. For many, the usual routine of getting ready for work, heading out for the morning commute, going for a quick walk to pick up lunch or to do a little shopping is gone. Many of us now spend a good part of our day in our homes, only venturing out for necessities.

Proving there is a direct correlation between fitness and COVID-19 immunity may be challenging. However, past studies have illustrated that physical activity protects against respiratory illnesses. The importance of exercise is often overlooked and is one of the best ways to keep our immune systems functioning at optimal levels. Such activity need not be vigorous or continuous. Health professionals suggest that 30 minutes of aerobic exercise 3-5 times per week is sufficient to maintain a reasonable level of health for the average person. That activity includes walking (though one should accelerate their pace to get the heart beating a little faster).

More rigorous regular exercise like running, cycling, and strength training, will help maintain and build muscle mass, increase bone density, and keep our immune systems healthy and able to fight off most viruses. Epidemiological studies show that people with moderate levels of physical activity have significantly fewer upper respiratory tract infections per year than less-active people. Regular exercise is also great for our mental health and reduces stress, especially during these challenging times.

People with higher immunity risk can benefit from exercise with its immunity-boosting blood flow. Sitting for long periods has become something of a reality for those working from home, so setting your smartwatch to remind you to stand up can keep the blood circulating. Beyond exercise, a day of rest and deep/REM sleep after active workouts can be beneficial to give your body time to recover.

For those used to going to the gym, playing tennis or going to a yoga class, working out and staying active at home and in isolation is not only boring but can be a challenge and difficult to stay motivated. Virtual classes and trainers can fill the void for some, but many miss the community atmosphere of working out with others, competing in a team sport, or tackling the climbing wall at the local gym. With many fitness facilities still shut down, many of us have given up our regular exercise routine.

For me, cycling and strength training is more than just a benefit to my physical health; it also benefits my mental health and helps me cope during stressful times.

Start with any activity you can. Even a little regular exercise will go a long way in helping you stay healthy during challenging times.

Chapter 10

Health Outcomes & AI

"We must think about personalized or individualized healthcare. We must consider individual responses to therapy and medication. There's nothing average when it comes to healthcare". – Geralyn Ochab, CEO of Imagia Inc.

Biotechnology or biotech, for short, is the broad area of biology, involving the use of living systems and organisms to develop or make products. Depending on the tools and applications, it often overlaps with related scientific fields. In the late 20th and early 21st centuries, biotechnology has expanded to include new and diverse sciences, such as genomics, recombinant gene techniques, applied immunology, and the development of pharmaceutical therapies and diagnostic tests.

Geralyn Ochab, the CEO of Imagia Inc., a healthcare imaging company, has always been interested in wellness and prevention. She firmly believes in people's ability to alter their circumstances through wellness routines and active prevention techniques.

Geralyn should know. As a career participant in the healthcare field, particularly in the application of technology to healthcare, she has seen many sides of the health equation. Ms. Ochab has travelled the globe, meeting experts from many countries and has been an executive leader in companies that pioneer in the healthcare field. Her current post has her leading a healthcare imaging company based in Montreal, Quebec, Canada that "brings together healthcare expertise and advanced artificial intelligence to diagnose, treat, and cure high burden diseases", which was one of the reasons we reached out to Geralyn, namely combining health and AI.

"These are really early days of artificial intelligence being applied to healthcare. There is so much potential, but it's not a magic wand of success, especially when the quality of data is far from guaranteed". Geralyn shares the story of Florence Nightingale, the pioneering nurse (and statistician) who, during the Crimean War, observed the link between sanitary conditions and mortality rate and forever altered clinical outcomes and saved lives. "With AI," she continues, "data hygiene is critical for medtech" to ensure we're using accurate, non-biased data to make diagnoses, assessments, and recommendations. "Data is heterogeneous, often messy, and not always structured. Healthcare and AI go well beyond the data available from your smartwatch. The industry must come together to progress the use of artificial intelligence in healthcare."

As we discussed global healthcare opportunities, Geralyn Ochab and I transitioned to personalized health, the primary focus of this book. "We must think about personalized or individualized healthcare. We must consider individual responses to therapy and medication. There's nothing average when it comes to healthcare". As we pointed out earlier in this book, it's interesting how consumers consistently lead other groups like IT teams, businesses, and government in the adoption of technology, and healthcare is no different. "Consumers are motivated towards improving their health," she continues, "and physicians who interact with them must understand how much access to their own data consumers now have and change their practice to adapt." We contend that consumers are increasingly taking healthcare into their own hands, given the barrage of information available, which will hopefully leave physicians to deal with more complex contraindications in the future.

One of the products that *Imagia* developed is called EVIDENS AI. It's described as a "discovery platform and clinical collaboration system" which allows for "federated learning" about data for patients across multiple hospitals, generating a basis for artificial intelligence and healthcare professionals, device makers, diagnostics manufacturers, pharma companies and more; to collaborate and generate new insights at a larger scale than traditional environments with a goal of greater personalized healthcare". Our complementary strengths in research and AI is a fierce combination that will spark the critical change needed for scientific discoveries, improved diagnostics, and more effective treatments resulting from new, scaled technologies," said Alexandre Le Bouthillier, Ph.D. Founder, Imagia.

Another AI-powered biotech company in the healthcare field is *Insilico Medicine*, which has developed a "comprehensive end-to-end drug discovery pipeline focused on helping people achieve greater longevity. Combining genomics, big data, and deep learning, *Insilico* analyzes how compounds affect cells and, by extension, what drugs can treat specific cells.

Leaders in the biotech longevity space include Peter Diamandis of XPrize and Singularity University fame, Jim Mellon (Founder and Chairman of Juvenescence), and Eric Verdin (MD, President, and CEO of the Buck Institute). They argue that preventative medicine, including ketogenesis (introducing a state of ketosis or metabolic state characterized by elevated levels of ketone bodies in the blood or urine), is key to extending healthspan. In this case, the body burns fat instead of carbohydrates triggering the production of anti-inflammatory ketone bodies.

Another use of biotechnology for longevity is using biomarkers. Given the vast increase in data availability, and more specifically, those that relate to aging, companies like Insilico Medicine can leverage insights to develop new biotechnology. Artificial intelligence provides the vehicle for processing/analysing the data, generating new insights for aging research.

Rather than using a single data type, i.e. age of parents, to develop predictions for longevity, deep learning can incorporate numerous factors including diseases, genetic makeup, microbiome, imaging, and much more. For those who want to understand their biological age better, AI has the potential to keep your own unique clock up-to-date, thus allowing the user to tweak their behaviours to increase their longevity potential.

When it comes to longevity, medical practitioners identify a potential disease state or health decline through biomarkers from simple measures like body mass index to the length of telomeres (the ends of chromosomes that shorten as humans age). By monitoring such measurements on a 24/7 basis, through a variety of sensors, consumers or patients could more accurately understand their ageing process.

Artificial intelligence enters the picture in its' ability to ingest, analyse, and summarize the billions of data points being offered up through these sensors. Summaries that could make decisions on medication, treatments, and therapies even more accurate than using traditional methods today.

Kaminskiy (Frontiers in AI) argues that only very sophisticated algorithms, like those associated with artificial intelligence, could provide both longevity insights at the global and individual level. Such precision insights could lead to preventive medicine, and support of longevity in humans.

Regeneration

Is it possible that as you age that you can improve your health? What about regenerating cells? Certain animals can regrow limbs. What about humans? Can we regenerate, and what does it take to regenerate?

Eyesight is a good example. As we age, we are told that failing eyesight is inevitable. Yet if you maintain your health at an optimal level, are you merely slowing degradation, or can you regenerate your cells through your health and diet?

Medical conditions like presbyopia, or progressive deterioration in the ability to observe close objects, naturally occur in people, particularly after the age of 60. Cataracts are common among seniors, and today can be corrected through surgery. Diabetic retinopathy and macular degeneration, however, are considered more serious and life-altering diseases.

Certainly, diet, exercise, non-smoking and periodic eye exams are traditional defenses against such diseases. However, new research into cellular reprogramming suggests startling possibilities in terms of regeneration and resetting older cells to more youthful status. Mice are the preliminary vectors of the de-aging effort; however, the question becomes how long before humans could benefit from younger cells.

The study we are referring to, conducted by David Sinclair and colleagues, following that study done at the Salk Institute in 2016, used partial cellular reprogramming on cells that alter during the aging process in mice.

Regeneration is the opposite of what the human body does naturally or degeneration. Cells and tissue degrade over time and the cause is the focus of many ongoing studies. In the Sinclair et al. study, they proposed that "accumulation of epigenetic noise" or disruption of youthful genes could be the cause of aging. While the study goes into great detail about aging and aging clocks, essentially, the opportunity exists where "old tissues retain a faithful record of youthful epigenetic information that can be accessed for functional age reversal." An exciting new opportunity emerges in which conducting partial cellular reprogramming to humans could reverse aging in human cells.

Artificial intelligence, and its ability to digest and analyse massive amounts of data, is ideal for the cellular reprogramming opportunity. Sequencing DNA used to consume years of computer time, and now a person's DNA can be sequenced in a day. AI makes that process more cost-effective, accurate, and faster than in the past, improving the opportunity to understand individual genetic blueprints better. Activities, whether within mice or humans, can be accessed. Susceptibility to disease, the impact of food types, and mutations can all be assessed for a unique human genome. With 20,000 genes and 3 billion base pairs of genetic letters, sequencing is a complex task, ready-made for the talents of artificial intelligence. Combining that capability with advances in cellular reprogramming, our eyes could be just one of many parts of our bodies that benefit from getting younger. Continued studies through Harvard's Personal Genome Project and the American Gut Microbiome project offers hope for more significant insights in the future.

Changing Cost of Drug Development via AI

When the range of cost to develop a new drug is between $2.5 billion and $12 billion, spent over a period of 10 years on average, and 90% of those drugs never actually make it market, pharma companies are highly motivated to reduce the time to successful product development. When 12% of the world's population will be over the age of 65 by 2030, many global citizens are running out of time for a medical answer.

The convergence of artificial intelligence, massive pharmacological datasets, 5G, and cloud storage (not to mention quantum computing) represents an opportunity for the pharmaceutical industry like never before. To develop new drugs in a fraction of the time, getting medication in the hands of those who need them sooner. Some estimates are up to 100 times faster, cheaper, and more appropriately focused.

Where is the data coming from? Text, images, online records, healthcare companies, medical devices, consumer devices, wearables like smartwatches, and public sources.

Antibiotics

Antibiotic and gene research are benefiting from artificial intelligence too. Nature Research suggests machine learning that can scan pools of 100 million molecules to support the creation of brand

117

antibiotics from scratch. My alma mater, Massachusetts Institute of Technology (MIT), recently used machine learning to screen 100 million molecules in just three days to discover halicin. This powerful new antibiotic can "kill many species of antibiotic-resistant bacteria." James Collins, the Termeer Professor of Medical Engineering and Science in MIT's Institute for Medical Engineering and Science (IMES) and Department of Biological Engineering said "We wanted to develop a platform that would allow us to harness the power of artificial intelligence to usher in a new age of antibiotic drug discovery...our approach revealed this amazing molecule, which is arguably one of the more powerful antibiotics that has been discovered." "The machine learning model can explore, in silico, large chemical spaces that can be prohibitively expensive for traditional experimental approaches," says Regina Barzilay, the Delta Electronics Professor of Electrical Engineering and Computer Science in MIT's Computer Science and Artificial Intelligence Laboratory (CSAIL).

In the healthcare field, artificial intelligence has become synonymous with medical diagnoses, including radiology, identifying cancerous growths or tumours, for example, that otherwise would not be evident to a human doctor by synthesizing massive volumes of patient data.

When it comes to heart attacks and strokes, AI functions as a hyper-detector as well. A group of researchers led by Kristopher Knott from the British Heart Foundation conducted a study, the largest of its kind up to 2020, published in *Circulation*, involving a process called CMRI or cardiovascular magnetic resonance imaging, combined with AI.

Measuring the blood flow to the heart, CMRI detects the amount of special contrast agent the heart muscle picks up, with stronger blood flow, meaning less likelihood of vessel blockages. By applying AI to the analysis (which is otherwise highly time-consuming and subject to human interpretation), the research team applied image recognition to the scans, teaching the AI what to look for (i.e. compromised blood flow) in the images. As a result of the research (that followed patients for 20 months), they determined a high degree of accuracy and that "for every 1 ml/g/min decrease in blood flow to the heart, the risk of dying from a heart event nearly doubled, and the risk of having a heart attack, stroke or other events more than doubled." By using this outcome regarding blood flow, researchers can now predict (along with other patient data) which patients are at higher risk of heart attacks and strokes.

Chapter 11

Health Practitioners and AI

"It is much more important to know what sort of a patient has a disease than what sort of a disease a patient has." – Sir William Osler

When discussing or sharing your information with your traditional MD versus a functional medicine doctor or naturopath, many of us often experience what is called "white coat syndrome." For too many of us, our appointments last only 5-10 minutes (excluding the long wait times). The Doctor asks a few questions, then types comments into electronic records, spends more time on the computer than talking to you, and not enough time to look at your deep health data.

For example, a doctor may be quick to prescribe medication then any spikes from overindulging on occasion in unhealthy food choices may result in more medication being recommended rather than the patient choosing not to overindulge or choosing food alternatives and monitoring their behaviour.

The predictive capability of AI-supported sensors (i.e. implants or nanobots) could be used as a post-consumption early warning of unhealthy food consumption. It would predict your blood sugar spike rather than waiting for post-spike. Some are more comfortable than others, especially if it provides the same data as your smartphone or smartwatch. Some only focus on certain data types (i.e. diabetes) and prefer others to track all of your data (assuming the data is secure) despite the fine print.

People choose their priorities. During the COVID-19 period, most would have said they want a constant virus monitor, to self-quarantine sooner. The same would be true of most viruses and colds. Many have been asymptomatic (not knowing they have the virus) so if the monitor alerts you then you can take whatever corrective action. Better than having a vaccine that is not always effective.

Today's media is awash with stories about insurance companies and their treatment of customers data, or requesting newly available data from new technology, and potentially using the same to terminate one's plan or increase their premiums based on information shared with them or your doctor.

Cancer is a perfect example of constant monitoring of the progress of the disease. Identifying cancerous cells like prostate-specific antigens (PSA) to determine whether a patient has cancer or is in remission. Insurance decisions today are based on actuarial tables to predict future events rather than constant monitoring.

In Rob's case, as part of routine checkups, PSA levels were monitored every two years. In 2013 Rob's PSA levels were normal, and in the follow-up visit in 2015, PSA levels had spiked. It was only then that the Doctor suspected something. Maybe it was a false positive? Unfortunately, in Rob's case, a biopsy confirmed cancer, resulting in lifesaving operation. Postoperative checkups are required regularly (3 months, 6 months, then annually). Fortunately for Rob, PSA levels remain undetectable 5-year post-operation. However, testing is onerous, scheduling trips to the laboratory for blood work, waiting for results and then booking time with the Doctor for follow up. Rob's Doctor has started to streamline this process and has developed an app (NED) that allows patients and doctors to share information about their health status. Using smart-tech apps will streamline this process and provide Doctors and patients with an increased exchange in the information.

Doctors can interpret the results of a blood test better than an untrained individual. They should do so. But that discussion can happen virtually as well.

Misdiagnosis

The leading causes of death in the United States and Canada are heart disease followed by cancer, but the third most leading cause may surprise you. Medical misdiagnosis & accidents are next on the list, both countries with more than 250,000 per year and 28,000 per year, respectively!

So, if AI were to err 1 in 10 million diagnoses, would that not be better? AI is expected to cut down on medical misdiagnosis. Autonomous cars are going through a similar period where the number of fatalities produced by self-driving cars per millions of miles compared to traditional fossil fuels cars is significantly less as AI does not get drunk, tired or distracted. There's lots more work to do in that area before humans are comfortable with autonomous cars ubiquitously on our roads, but there is a case to be made. The same case for applying AI to medical diagnoses. (MOVE?)

Medical applications like *Ada* offer communication with the user providing medical recommendations about symptoms, complaints and which doctor to visit or remote consultation to follow-up. Other medical solutions like *Lunit* use machine learning and 3D visualization software, increasing the probability of detecting lung, airway and breast cancer by over 80%. *Sense.ly* monitors those who recently underwent long-term treatment or suffered chronic diseases and provided recommendations and specialist referrals. PathAI, founded by a Harvard Med School graduate, helps doctors more timely diagnose complex diseases through machine learning and cell image analysis. *Aira* is a service that connects blind and low vision people with live remote agents, or the Artificial Intelligence agent referred to as Chloe, to help blind people read instructions, for example, on a medicine bottle.

MedTech

You may have heard about the Internet of Things or IoT, a phenomenon where billions of sensors, integrated into millions of everyday devices worldwide, deliver data to the internet, providing information instantaneously. The Internet of Medical Things (IoMT) is a similarly large subcomponent of the IoT. Estimated to be worth over $50 billion by 2022, consumers and medical technology companies are taking advantage of interconnected devices and an incredible capability to deliver new streams of healthcare analysis, diagnosis and solutions.

Patient Engagement & Adherence

All the data, analysis and recommendations in the world will not guarantee that a user, consumer or patient will follow up with sustained action. Often referred to as the "last mile of healthcare," engagement usually means the difference between success and failure of a health or fitness program. As authors of this book, we know from first-hand experience that it takes a great deal of work to improve your health. Determination, passion, persistence aren't just buzz words – they help you get out of bed and into the gym or onto the bicycle. Adherence to a fitness program almost always gains positive results.

Healthcare practitioners provide their expertise in developing a care plan. Personal trainers offer fitness programs, and dieticians offer a meal plan to address the patient or client objectives. Not complying with these plans and programs means failure to reach those objectives. One study of over 300 leaders of clinics and healthcare units determined that most patients were not highly engaged.

So how can artificial intelligence help? Nudging, for example, is an ideal use of artificial intelligence. Identifying objectives, learning your behaviour, providing alerts, observing outcomes, nudging you again are all tactics to improve the patient's or client's adherence level to care plans and coach or trainer programs. Apple Watch has a feature that nudges (reminds) you to stand every hour. Apps that provide rewards like completed fitness circles or badges when you complete an activity can motivate some. All of your collected data is stored on your smartphone (e.g. Apple Health App) and then sent to your medical professional. Apple EGC feature allows you to send a .pdf file to your cardiologist. These approaches can increase adherence in a healthcare environment.

SECTION 2   DEEP HEALTH

Chapter 12

What is Artificial Intelligence?

"Some people call this artificial intelligence, but the reality is this technology will enhance us. So instead of artificial intelligence, I think we'll augment our intelligence."- Ginni Rometty, former CEO of IBM

When I started my business, Aquitaine Innovation Advisors, back in 2017, I set one primary mission. I wanted to help companies worldwide go beyond merely understanding AI, scaling up their organizations using the power of artificial intelligence, and doing so ethically.

In 2017, very few organizations were having success in implementing AI within their business. My objective was to help these groups (this included companies in financial services, retail, construction, and even technology) overcome barriers and achieve the same level of revenue growth, profit, and customer satisfaction that only a small portion of businesses achieve.

At the time, few understood what artificial intelligence was, let alone how they could use it within their organizations. Our objective in Section 2 of this book is to share what AI is, how you can use it to improve your health and fitness levels, and share exciting new things the future has in store for you!

Early Days

The first dozen companies I worked with, who stated they wanted to understand better what AI was and how it could be used, did not pursue AI beyond the first meeting. Now maybe you think I wasn't persuasive enough, and there could be some truth to that. Yet, each leader I spoke to inevitably worried how AI would distract their teams from core activities and revenues, how many risks were involved, and how few projects succeeded. All those issues were valid, yet each could be overcome, and the potential rewards were overwhelming.

As you read this book, I hope you come to understand how you can use artificial intelligence to improve something about yourself now and how it will become increasingly possible. The magic of artificial intelligence is not in coding. It's in the imagination of humans. Let's explore that imagination. Let's start with the history of artificial intelligence.

History of AI

While we could travel back to the 1830s when Charles Babbage and Ada Lovelace developed the first design for a programmable machine, AI begins around 1943. Warren McCulloch and colleague Walter Pitts drew parallels between the human brain and computing machines to create neural networks (emulating how the human brain thinks).

In 1950, British mathematician and statistician Alan Turing introduced a way to test a machine's intelligence by creating the Turing test. Essentially the idea was could you determine that the machine was, in fact, a machine within the first five minutes. Remember, even today's AI can only perform specific tasks, and none can do all the

127

things a human can do. By 1955, the term artificial intelligence had been coined by a group of academics at Dartmouth University.

Fast forward to the 1980s when Edward Feigenbaum created systems that emulated human experts' decisions. By 1997, IBM's computer program called Deep Blue was beating a world chess champion, Garry Kasparov, for the first time. The first self-driving car for urban conditions, which uses AI, was built in 2009 by Google. IBM came to the public eye again in 2011 when its computer program, Watson, beat the Jeopardy champions. No doubt, you or someone you know uses Siri or some other personal assistant – which came to the market in 2014 using speech recognition to answer questions and perform rudimentary tasks. Back to the game world, Google's AlphaGo defeated the world Go champion, Lee Sedol, in 2016. By 2018, most universities had an artificial intelligence course on their curriculum.

Much has been made in the media about the Fourth Industrial Revolution (following the industrial, electricity, and computer revolutions). As a result of advances in computing power, cloud storage, processing speeds, and AI, it becomes increasingly easier to collect, analyse, and offer insights and health recommendations. Collecting data such as the types we discussed in Section 1 can provide individual groups and global entities insights into ourselves and our populations.

Artificial intelligence will be its engine, data its fuel, IoT its data collectors or fuel system, and computing infrastructure its vehicle, leading to robust new ideas and solutions for a healthier life.

The bulk of the progress in AI has happened in the last five years, and in good measure because of the avalanche of fuel for artificial intelligence. That being data. Some sources suggest over 90% of the world's data has been produced in the last two years, and that 90% marker is moving ever more into one year as more sensors are being unleashed every day.

What is Artificial Intelligence?

Let's begin with the basics. In its simplest definition, Artificial Intelligence is the attempt by humans to emulate the human brain - the best-known data processor. The human brain uses synapse connections to transfer information between neurons in different brain regions to process things like visual images, physical balance, auditory activity, and communication.

I recall I was inspired by a New York Times article by Craig S. Smith that was shared by a colleague to explain artificial intelligence. After reading the article, I wanted to see if, after years of being entrenched in AI, I could still explain the topic to a 10-year old. Smith pointed out in his article out that "When a mother points to a dog and tells her baby, 'Look at the doggy,' the child learns what to call the furry four-legged friend. That is supervised learning."

Based on that description, I took it further. If the same child were given a cookie in reward for correctly identifying yet another object as a dog (let's say the first dog was a Labrador and the second dog was a collie), then that would be reinforcement learning. If the child were to do this, over and over again (in the case of artificial intelligence, a scale of millions of times) telling the mother how likely each image was a dog, this would be called machine learning. That is, in essence, what artificial intelligence is—teaching a machine to learn. And a sample of one 10-year old understood this explanation.

The figure below illustrates the basics of AI. Data or the input is fed into an algorithm (a set of lines of computer code). Through the advances in computer processing speed, storage growth, cloud capabilities, global investment, and talent, the data is processed repeatedly by machine learning technology. As the data is processed, the computer begins to learn. The more data (especially clean, accurate, unbiased data), the more learning occurs, and the higher the potential accuracy level of the algorithm.

The Basics of Artificial Intelligence

Source: Brian Lenahan

The output (y) is the objective of the process. What you want to determine. For example, a pharma industry company wants to develop a new drug to combat a virus. By entering all available, relevant data into the algorithm and running millions of scenarios in a shorter period of time than human trials would take, the company develops many options for a viable vaccine, each with a greater likelihood of success, the more layers that are in the machine learning algorithms.

Data, which can come in vast volumes, can be images, text, voice, and more. Since AI started in the 1950s, AI has increasingly been able to learn, which learning comes in many forms. As illustrated in the story told to the 10-year old, by repetition (layers and layers of algorithms or combinations of logic and code), through rewards (think a robot moving through a maze), through comparison (think chocolate cookie comparison to a chihuahua), and other forms of learning.

Machine learning, a subset of AI refers to data analysis tools that can extract insights without specific programming like traditional computers. It is this ability to intake vast amounts of data and generate insights that powers the tools laid out in this book. By learning from history, whether that be what food you ate, how many laps of the track you ran, or the beating of your heart, machine learning can extract patterns or insights that humans would be unable to observe and do it faster.

When I work with leaders of large corporations and entrepreneurs of scaling tech firms, we often talk about not what AI is but also what it can do for them. You will see throughout this book examples of what AI can do for you. It's an incredible time to be alive and take advantage of AI to support your health, nutrition, and fitness goals.

Striving to Be Better Using AI

The opportunity humans have for the use of artificial intelligence is staggering. We want to be better in so many ways. We inherently want to feel better, look better, and achieve more. When you know yourself better, you have a greater chance of achieving such goals.

That's the purpose of this book. To help you, collect and use data points about yourself, throw them into an AI algorithm and generate some real insights about yourself.

When I speak to large groups, whether they be business leaders, students, consultants, or AI enthusiasts, I always talk about the importance of human/AI hybrid solutions. By that, I mean, almost every process, operation, or activity I encounter is done best through a combination of people and technology. Take, for example, a call center. Humans historically were the initiators and recipients of phone calls. Today, bots, whether text or voice chatbots, are capable of rudimentary conversation with a human client or user. It's essential that call centers have such capability given people worldwide have moved quickly to mobile apps and text or voice, and they are doing that in huge numbers. Yet when it comes to complex calls, call centers refer those to a human, and rightly so given the key attribute of empathy humans possess. We often deal with automated call agents or chatbots, which are powered by lots of data and AI algorithms. They're all over the internet, in your home, and on your smartphone. The more you speak to them, the smarter they become because you've given them more data to learn from.

AI is often thought of as eliminating human interaction, yet using it as a tool to improve or augment these interactions, thereby taking our human capabilities to the next level, is our goal. People can best equip themselves for the accelerating onslaught of AI and machine learning systems by learning to partner with them. *Artificial Intelligence: Foundations for Business Leaders & Consultants,* my first book, guided that audience through the definitions, concepts and that learning and partnering process. ***Deep Health*** seeks to guide you through a path of better health for longer using artificial intelligence.

As an executive in a Top 10 North American financial institution, I witnessed the evolution of artificial intelligence within a large corporate environment. As a student at MIT, I learned from leading professors and a cohort of over 500 colleagues around the world about AI strategy and how AI was changing the face of the planet. As an AI strategy expert, I want to share my experience, academic learning and research with you. In researching ***Deep Health***, I was fascinated by the incredible momentum globally in developing more and more AI solutions for extending the health span of humans. From all corners of the globe, exciting new developments provide new insights through the aggregation of data about millions upon millions of humans wearing watches, clothing, implantable devices, etc., and translating that data into how the body functions and how we can strive to become even better.

The future holds incredible opportunities for AI. Some believe that AI will make us less human or consume our society. That is one possible future. There will also be opportunities to support human interaction and solve humanity's most significant challenges. By reading this book, we hope that by embracing artificial intelligence and smart technology, you will be better able to prepare yourself for developments in physical and mental fitness and health in general.

AI & Longevity Organizations

Around the world, we see significant interest and progress regarding longevity. For example, the AI for Longevity Summit or ALS organised by Aging Research at King's (ARK) and AI Longevity Consortium at King's College London, supported by Biogerontology Research Foundation, Aging Analytics Agency, and Deep Knowledge Ventures.

The convergence of artificial intelligence and longevity becomes evident in the significant increase in research in the two now-related fields. It's happening in academia and industry. The consortium brings these fields together to enable sharing and technology transfer, applying deep learning techniques to research in longevity factors, whether for drug discovery, therapeutics, and social science applications.

Among ALS's objectives are to accelerate the diagnosis of age-related health decline, healthy ageing biomarkers, development of personalized health practices, and promotion of healthy lifestyles. As AI and biomedicine for longevity converge, the probability of shifting to hyper-personalized preventive care increases.

We all want to live longer and healthier. Today, in laboratories and research centers around the world, there is significant anti-aging research taking place. Healthcare is garnering some of the highest investments in artificial intelligence, according to CB Insights. Start-ups in the field collected $1.6 billion in new investments in just one quarter of 2019.

One of the foremost researchers in the longevity field is David Sinclair, Ph.D. author of *Lifespan – Why We Age and Why We Don't Have To*. This type of research would take years to gather and analyze the datasets if not for advanced technology, massive computing power, and Artificial Intelligence (AI). There are recent discussions about AI support to reverse-aging.

Interest in the field of longevity is growing. In 2019, the Silicon Valley incubation program Y Combinator put out a call to provide seed funding for extending longevity. Other AI-powered companies looking for longevity interventions are Juvenescence.AI, Longevity Vision Fund, and Life Biosciences.

AI Communities for Good

Over 15 years ago, Dragos Ionel was convinced to come to Canada from Romania. He and his wife Monica brought along their respective expertise to share with Canadian companies. Dragos was inspired by the type of technology being developed in the Canadian arena, especially that related to artificial intelligence. Being the social type he is, it made sense to gather together like-minded, passionate people to talk about this burgeoning technology area.

He formed AIGeeks, a community with over 4,000 members, and some incredible sponsors like RBC, Deloitte and more. Due to Dragos' passion for artificial intelligence and his persistence in making a community thrive, the AIGeeks community met monthly to full, standing room only sessions with two or three speakers on diverse AI topics.

Given its leadership in AI research and training, the Greater Toronto area pulses with anticipation for what the future will bring with artificial intelligence. My inspiration is supporting the development of an environment where Canada will lead in these two areas and implementation. And where Canadian companies are starting to make those in-roads, the AIGeeks community of experts and enthusiasts will play a crucial role.

Now Dragos has a second-generation involved in the AI community, namely his daughter and steering committee member, Andrea Ionel. I interviewed Andrea for one of my books on AI transitions (how students, and those new to the workforce, can successfully transition into the world of artificial intelligence, preparing for roles that don't even exist yet). Andrea is an eloquent, enthusiastic high school student who has seen the opportunity that AI offers and embraced the organization that her father and others founded.

After seeing organizations like AIGeeks community growth, it will be fascinating to see what happens next, and who else will be attracted to this AI group in the future. Organizations like this one can be leaders in the implementation of *Deep Health*.

Facing the Realities of AI Head-on

In the fall of 2019, I had the privilege of speaking at an **AIGeeks** Meetup Session in Toronto, sharing my thoughts on AI strategies. The audience, composed of AI experts and enthusiasts, focused predominantly on how artificial intelligence was being used in projects. The presentations focused on strategies to improve the likelihood of the "AI for Good," like reducing food waste or supporting those with disabilities.

It was apparent when my message hit the mark when smartphones were raised in the air to snap photos of my slides. In particular, one slide: Facing the Realities of AI Head On. When a large percentage of AI projects fail (some sources suggest as high as 70%), it is crucial to understand which tactics and strategies the successful projects deploy. So, I shared my Top 5 strategies.

People – the highest percentage of AI initiatives fail not because of the technology but because of people. Incompatibility amongst team members, lack of organizational commitment to AI, and lack of team diversity contribute to extended timelines, cost overruns, and poor execution. For example, diversity should not be limited to data scientists, data engineers, and business leaders or SME's. Gender, age, and specialty diversity keep the team engaged with new ideas and broad context for their projects. Adding artists to the team, for example, can provide incredible creativity that would otherwise not be available to rules-based thinkers.

Human Oversight – whenever I speak with groups that are not involved in the technology day-to-day, they recoil from the idea of artificial intelligence making decisions or taking actions without human oversight. And with good cause. Bias, accuracy, security, false positives, brand impacts…the list goes on and on. Having humans oversee processes is a sound approach, and as an AI practitioner, pitching a solution without that oversight dooms many projects.

Regulation - As I've written about in the past, AI regulation is immature. The EU's GDRP, the National Institute of Science and Technology (NIST) in the US, and the Digital Charter in Canada all seek to regulate artificial intelligence activities. Yet, such regulations or guidelines have only been developed or published in the last two years. Hardly long enough to make artificial intelligence cases a staple in our judicial systems. For those companies deploying AI, being able to explain precisely what the "black box" is doing can go a long way to satisfying the demands of those regulatory agencies. We discuss regulation in greater detail in the appendices.

Push-back - Facial recognition is extensively used in the Chinese ecosystem, yet recently has been banned in San Francisco and Oakland, and sweeping regulation is planned for the EU. Deepfakes, especially of humans that don't exist (the detail and creativity are frightening), are pushing the dark side of artificial intelligence every day. Being aware of the technology categories that are receiving push-back and in which geographies can inform your AI strategy decisions.

Responsible AI – TD Bank, a large North American Bank, led a 2019 Responsible AI forum where experts discussed how organizations should consider biases, accuracy, privacy, and human oversight. Most consulting firms have expounded on Responsible AI (RAI). As described by the World Economic Forum, the four keys to deploying RAI are governance (clear ethical and accountability standards), design (creativity that aligns with governance and makes the process transparent), monitoring (auditing against your RAI metrics) and reskilling (democratizing the understanding of AI across the organization). Increasingly AI partners and customers will expect clear RAI structure from their AI vendors.

Trillions of dollars are being poured into AI globally, and this trend is highly likely to continue. Coming up with the next great artificial intelligence algorithm or machine learning concept is only part of the battle. To win, drivers of artificial intelligence need to deploy strategies that focus on increasing the potential to be responsible, ethical market winners.

Chapter 13

Health Data Apps

"On pure speculation, just an educated guess, I'd say that man is alive." – Dr. Leonard McCoy to Spock, Star Trek

On television's Star Trek, Dr. Leonard McCoy, in almost every episode he appeared in, produced a device to diagnose his patients. The electronic whirr of the device was unique, and its capabilities were legendary—the medical tricorder. A combined scanner and analysis device, the medical tricorder, a handheld portable device, could make a diagnosis within seconds of activation.

While such a device remains in 23rd-century fiction, many have tried to create the tricorder, including those who chased the X-Prize for this device starting in 2012.

In 2018, the winner of the X-Prize was an AI-powered prototype called ***DxtER***. In terms of functionality, ***DxtER*** incorporated a chest sensor, spirometer, digital stethoscope, blood pressure calibrator, and wrist sensor into one device. This device can detect over 34 medical conditions, including pneumonia, hypertension, COPD, anemia, bronchitis and asthma. All the data is fed into a central AI program for medical diagnoses.

While DxtER represents an incredible advance over previous versions of the tricorder, we envision a much more robust **Deep Health** model that incorporates all of the elements discussed in an earlier chapter.

As two people consumed by the topic of anti-aging, we get together every week at Starbucks to talk about the subjects of nutrition, fitness and anti-aging. In those discussions, we always learn something new about the impact of food choice, fitness and artificial intelligence on aging. Yet we also occasionally became overwhelmed by it all.

Is there such a thing as too much data? As humans, we can become overwhelmed with millions of pieces of data coming at us on which to make decisions that affect our health. On the other hand, what's the difference between having 30 bits of data or 300? How much does your knowledge improve? How much, relatively, does your health improve by acting on that data? AI functions on the weighting of factors generating probabilities and real-life parallels. By adding weights to various scenarios through its learning process, AI can emulate reality. It can also allow you to set priorities for factors that go into your health based on the level of impact and importance. Another benefit of having a **Deep Heath** model is that AI can stop you from being overwhelmed.

What was also frustrating for us was that, as we came into contact with more products and services, we needed numerous apps to collect the data (food analysis from a visual scanner, weight information from a scale, DNA data from a third party, fitness activities from a smartwatch, etc.). Our real interest was in a solution that integrated all of our data, analysed it, and provided recommendations. It sounds very much like what artificial intelligence can do.

The more we talked about it, the more we thought of the concept of *Deep Health*. The ability to link all of the available (and future) data sources into one data repository that can help you optimize your choices for longevity and healthspan. The *Deep Health* concept would focus one's data collection into a unique, highly accurate, real-time device attached to you or forms part of you. Intrigued?

Artificial intelligence offers us the opportunity to take vast quantities of data; in this case, personal data, and perform analysis that humans could not otherwise accomplish. When you consider the billions of cells in our bodies, trillions of elements in our microbiome, thousands of food choices and nutrients, and hundreds of activities, it would be impossible to assess the interaction of all the variables you could understand. The combinations and permutations are too great. But not for artificial intelligence.

Deep Health does not exist today (yet); however, in this book, we provide the conceptual possibilities for some talented innovators to pursue helping humankind live healthier, longer lives. *Healthspan Data Aggregation & Recommendation* or *HDAR* is our concept for combining food science, nutrition, fitness and physiology. The diagram below provides an example of how HDAR could work with your unique information. The various elements, including food, your biome, blood components, DNA, etc. are inputs to the process (identified with an 'x'). The algorithm analyses the data elements and provides insight into your specific circumstances. Based on controls your select, it recommends what steps to take next to continue toward your goals or population benchmarks (like Body Mass Index, for example).

The first component of the **Deep Health** model is the Healthspan Data Aggregation or HDA module. Data combined from the fields of food science, nutrition, fitness, biology and physiology are aggregated into a data pool under appropriate licenses, covering both general populations through public or private databases and personal data collected close to you. For example, through its purchase of Fitbit, organizations like Google have obtained a massive fitness data source to leverage into personalized products and services for consumers. HDAR would aggregate your medical records, smartwatch data, brainwave patterns, daily schedules, environmental impacts, nutritional content and more, storing data in a cloud environment with strict privacy controls. Diagram 1 below illustrates the concept. Remember, this our concept, not an actual offering in planning or production today.

Health & AI

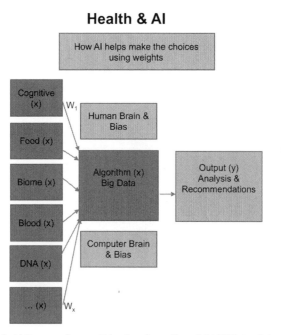

Diagram 1 – Health & AI Process - Source: Brian Lenahan – Copyright 2020 Aquitaine Innovation Advisors

142

The second module is the *Deep Health* Recommendation module or DHR. Within the DHR module, artificial intelligence is applied to your trend data. It is then compared to the greater population and then offers personalized recommendations that take into account all of the interactions gathered with the HDA. DHR can assess the materiality of each piece of data or category of data to you individually. The user can sift through various recommendations, consider those that are prioritized by the DHR and choose to apply them themselves or in concert with their healthcare practitioner. Recommendations can come in the form of text, voice or visuals.

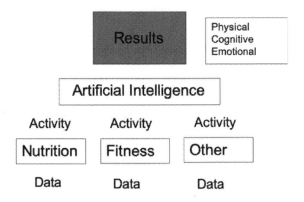

Diagram 2 – Deep Health Recommendation model - Source: Brian Lenahan – Copyright 2020 Aquitaine Innovation Advisors

The third component of the *Deep Health* model is the *Deep Health* Profile (DHP). AI can help us build a hyper-accurate DHP by using all or most of the data identified earlier in the book, moving us from a shallow understanding of our health to one of *Deep Health*. Individuals who integrate deep health into their lives need to have all that summarized in a way that is easy to understand and review regularly.

The chart's objective is to inform the user of their progress in applying knowledge gained through HDA and DHR. If we have learned anything from our experiences with collecting personal data, motivation is key, and progress is an incredible motivator. There is a clear relationship between how much knowledge you gain and how much action you take with the outcomes you achieve, so providing that view within your personal DHP is important.

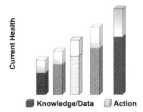

Diagram 3 – Deep Health Profile - Source: Brian Lenahan – Copyright 2020 Aquitaine Innovation Advisors

By leveraging AI and data, one can gain insights into their fitness, nutrition, and cognitive state, resulting in a Deep Health Profile. The *Deep Health* model envisions a user interface that offers a summary view of this dynamic and detailed drill-downs for each component.

In terms of their physiology and preferences, every individual is different, so we envision malleable, customizable interfaces to drive the regular interactions with the device.

We can't be sure when such a device will be available. Still, the next chapter will offer insights into technology that will super-charge *Deep Health* for you and below, we provide some partial AI-powered solutions that exist today.

Applications like *Nutrino* combine various sources of information, which "uncovers the invisible connections between people and food to empower better nutritional decisions for better health

144

outcomes… *Nutrino* leverages state of the art data science, natural language processing and mathematical models from the worlds of optimization theory and predictive analytics."

iCarbonX is a solution that digitizes human life, collecting sample data, including air quality, saliva, diets, and fitness activities, to create a "digital you" based on your unique data. *iCarbonX* has designated their AI technology to search through individual's data to detect signals about longevity, health, and disease leading to product offerings personalized to the users' needs.

With their AI technology, *Buoy Health* uses different algorithms to diagnose and treat illness. Patients share their health concerns and symptoms to a chatbot that will guide them to the appropriate cure based on its diagnosis. *Buoy Health* is used by many hospitals and healthcare providers, including Harvard Medical School.

The *Cleveland Clinic* is a world-renowned hospital that has partnered with IBM to use AI to simplify the patient experience. By linking AI with data collection to gather information on trillions of administrative and health record data points, Cleveland Clinic helps personalize healthcare individually.

Tempus is a company with the goal of using AI to help physicians identify treatments and cures, by sifting through the world's most extensive collection of clinical and molecular data to personalize healthcare treatments. Tempus is developing AI tools that collect and analyze various data types, from genetic sequencing to image recognition. Their current focus is on AI-driven cancer research and treatments.

Google's software is being used by global hospitals to help move patients from testing to treatment more efficiently. Doctors can use the **DeepMind** Health program to collect patients' symptoms and store them in a massive data library. This helps doctors with the diagnostic stage by sifting through the dataset for comparable symptoms. Also, the platform notifies doctors when a patient's health deteriorates.

Elevate is a brain training program that makes personalized adjustments for each individual the more you use it. This app includes daily brain games to improve transferable skills, like your speaking abilities and math skills.

MyFitnessPal is a fitness app that uses AI to help individuals track their progress related to their fitness goals. After entering your information, the app can help you identify reasonable fitness goals personalized for you while enabling you to track your diet and workout sessions. Also, individuals can connect with others in the *MyFitnessPal* community for extra motivation or advice.

ShopWell is a mobile app created to help you curate the perfect diet plan personalized to your needs and goals while providing efficient ways to follow your diet plan. The app includes a feature that allows you to scan a food label, offers a personalized nutrition rating/score for that food and recommends alternate food choices to help you find the best foods for your diet plan.

Record is a health and fitness app, created by Under Armour, that provides users with the ability to track sleep, fitness, activity, and nutrition all in one place. Along with this, Record allows users to connect and sync devices easily, and provides you with personalized health tips and connects you with other users.

FitGenie incorporates AI to generate personalized data related to calorie intake, to provide users with food suggestions. The app will help you adjust your macronutrients according to the data it collects, offering a highly customized nutrition plan.

Making Sense of it All

At some point in reading this book, you may be asking yourself how could I possibly absorb all the information Rob and Brian are directing my way? Not surprisingly, many have asked us that question already. Check out any "Best Smartwatches of 2020" list on the internet. Editors will describe a vast array of functions and preferences. How information is displayed is one of those criteria on their list. Simple starting points like is a square face better than a round face? (Rob's square Apple Watch face vs Brian's round Samsung Active Watch 2 face). Is the bezel on the outside or not? How is the quality of the touchscreen? Screen brightness. Is the screen always on? Dimming or blue light effectiveness? How easily does the data sync with your larger smartphone screen? Font size and colours? All that without even starting to consider what data is displayed to you and when.

Personalized news feeds like those available from Twitter or LinkedIn offer you data, unlike anyone else's. Similarly, smartwatches often you a unique set of data. Brian switches his watch face monthly to compare the visuals and data collection effectiveness. Periodic badges appear after every goal is achieved. Rob's a big fan of "completing the circles" on his Apple Watch for his activity goals. My watch reminds me to stand when I've been sitting too long (probably writing). It reminds me of UV levels. Sleep tracking is the first set of data that I look at every morning. All-in-all, it has taken me over a year to nail down what data I want to see consistently.

Progress in telling the story of the data we collect has been remarkable in the last decade. Yet it should be even more accessible and more comfortable, and those involved in that pursuit are increasing in number. Around the world, athletes, business and government leaders and technology types increasingly make the identical demand of their teams given the preponderance of data. A new role and field of study have emerged called data storytelling or data visualization to address this demand. People who study and excel at telling stories about data and with data. They attend conferences, such as the Open Data Science Conference in Europe or North America Data Virtualization streams, where they "explore the beauty of visualization brought to you by the world's most creative minds." These creative minds alter how we see, comprehend and interact with data through the art of storytelling using the most up-to-date open-source tools and techniques. What's their objective? "To create beautiful, insightful, and actionable data graphics and visuals."

Wouldn't you prefer an interactive interface that says, "Hey Brian, here's what all this means" in plain language? Rather than data that needs to be analysed and interpreted, common language assessment of your hyper-personalized data and a conversation with a virtual interface to discuss how you can optimize your health. Consider the case of Narrative Science, experts in data storytelling. *Narrative Science*, a 10-year old spinoff from Northwestern University lab, uses natural language processing to analyse data (text, numbers, voice, image) from numerous sources to create a data story in plain English. Although intended for business clients, the concept is the same for consumers. Tell me a story about me. Offer me more than a table, chart, graph or mass-market training video. Tell a story. Narrative Science's *Lexio* does just that for businesses. Reuters and other agencies do it to a certain extent, with their personalized online news.

Consumers need that for their health, receiving non-intuitive insights from all that collected data and Deep Health type vendors move in that direction.

The value of storytelling can be seen differently – as a reward. James Landay, professor of computer science at Stanford University and associate director of the Stanford Institute for Human-Centered Artificial Intelligence (Stanford HAI), led an effort to introduce storytelling rewards into one's fitness regime. Observing that people who wear smartwatches and bands view their results differently (in many cases as negative reinforcement of what they did not do), Landay decided that storytelling could help others achieve their fitness goals. So, he and a team of students developed 'Who Is Zuki'. This fitness app rewards users when they complete a goal by advancing them along in a story about Zuki (think ET travelling to Earth to find family).

How does the 'Zuki' app work? Every week, the story advances one chapter, on a synched smartphone, when the user completes their fitness goals. The objective? To encourage activity, the moment one opens up their smartphone. Tests showed that over three weeks, users were more engaged than a control group, excited in the knowledge they would be rewarded with learning more about Zuki's trials and adventures. The story is told mostly through visuals, progress indicators and combines fitness activities a user would relate to. When the test results were published, the publication was rewarded with the best paper at the Association for Computing Machinery's Conference on Human Factors in Computing Systems (CHI 2020). Landay expects to integrate story choices to broaden the appeal to a diverse fitness audience. Today, a more extensive study is underway, but the theory remains solid. Humans are naturally engaged in stories, especially those that build to a riveting climax.

Another example is the use of AI to create advertising and novels. Take the Lexus ad developed by feeding 15 years of award-winning advertisements to IBM's Watson. The result, a somewhat unoriginal ad but one resplendent in its display of AI's capabilities. Or the creation of a new Game of Thrones novel by Zach Thoutt using AI and previous volumes to predict what might happen next. Games like Fortnite, a dynamic story about a 'battle royale,' uses AI-driven bots as a method to train players, "behaving similarly to normal players … and as your skill improves, you'll face fewer bots," states Epic Games, Fortnite's creator. AI as part of online games, novel creation and advertising… all storytelling opportunities where the medium supports the message.

So, let's return to our concept of data storytelling. Data visualizers need to think about those engaged in Deep Health to be compelled to continue. Merely providing data is not enough. Closing a ring is good, but having a personalized story about one's efforts would keep the user more engaged, more often based on Landay's research. Developing Deep Health user interfaces to share commentary on nutrition choices and impacts, fitness activities, and body/mind improvements would augment the overall, lifelong experience. Instead of fictional characters, the user would be at the center of the story, with artificial intelligence using machine learning, natural language processing, and compelling visuals and voice to propel the user into a lifetime of Deep Health.

We acknowledge AI as a disruptive force and a significant opportunity. We recognize the importance of eliminating biases by any measure, including gender, race, period of time or other factors, and valuing individuals' privacy. Storytelling development must be cognizant of these and errors inherent in data to be practical to global populations. Application developers would be wise to ensure such controls are in place to be broadly accepted and embraced and train AI for diversity, ethics and responsibility. Notably, as well, the ability to make meaning of a person's data should not yet be the sole teller of the story. We do recommend the involvement of a healthcare practitioner in concert with the miracles of AI.

As Brian has said at many technology conferences, AI needs creative people as much as it requires technical people involved in its evolution. Such creatives applied to storytelling for fitness and health would explore human beings' sentimental and emotional reactions to stories. Using their gifts to develop Deep Health applications, combined with data storytellers, should alter the trajectory of smart wearable fitness types far into the future. Making meaning of trillions of pieces of data (think of the microbiome alone) is difficult for machines and impossible for humans. Crafting artificial intelligence to make meaning, translate and share our own story is expected to advance our healthspan journey.

The future is now and is changing faster than people think. The disruptive forces of big data and AI will change our healthcare systems and turn industries upside down. These changes will soon enable us to take control of our health in ways never before possible and help healthcare practitioners diagnose and treat disease. We will be able to customize our diets based on our DNA profiles and optimize our lifestyles to help us live longer, healthier lives.

Chapter 14

Technology of the Future

"Any sufficiently advanced technology is indistinguishable from magic." – Arthur C. Clarke

We started the journey for this book in early 2020 with a series of LinkedIn articles about sorting through and making sense of the superabundance of information available to the average consumer. If you could take all the data points we discussed in those articles (diet logs, weight, allergies, blood type, disease, microbiome, DNA, fitness stats, etc.) and have your smartphone make sense of them to form a comprehensive, personalized diet and fitness regime, would you be interested? What if you could test how those combinations reacted before you ingested something or tried a new activity?

Your Digital Twin

In the final article of the 2020 LinkedIn series, we introduced the concept of Healthspan Data Analysis & Recommendation or HDAR. HDAR, our term, refers to the collection of personalized health datasets (collating information about your genome, epigenome, food science, nutrition, fitness and physiology), entering them into an algorithm, and through the wonders of artificial intelligence provide recommendations on what to eat, when to eat it, and what to avoid (such as allergens), creating the best possible outcome for you. One way to accomplish this is through a digital twin. This sort of twin exists in the manufacturing sector, for example, to help research and development teams analyse their real-life assets (like GE's plane engines) in a risk-free way.

Digital twins, a virtual copy of a physical entity (animate or non-animate), are now possible given the convergence of so many technologies. IoT sensors for health and wellness applications have emerged, smart applications for wearable devices, massive amounts of data (shared or private), and advances in cloud computing and AI have resulted in the movement towards digital twin capabilities.

Between 2010 and 2020, sensor prices fell by 50%. Cloud computing became prevalent during this same period, and today is ubiquitous. Digital twins, leveraging these technologies and AI and 5G, will become indispensable tools for healthcare practitioners and individuals seeking to optimize their health and live longer. The Gartner Hype Cycle, an ongoing review of technology maturity, suggests that digital twins will be commonplace (reach the plateau of productivity) from 2022 onwards.

One might think it would be impossible to replicate a human being fully through complex sensor data, however consider the complexity of elements comprising a GE jet engine - subsonic inlets, supersonic inlets, compressors, combustors, turbines, afterburners (reheat), nozzles, thrust reversers, cooling systems, fuel systems, propellant pumps, engine starting system, ignition, lubrication system, and the control system. Highly sophisticated and measured by sensors.

153

Imagine, if you will, a twin of yourself in virtual space; a digital twin. A digital twin of the human body that considers all your data – blood type, DNA, height, weight, BMI, etc. – and allows you to adjust settings to see the relative impacts on your real body. Through the use of thousands of sensors, whether external (worn on the skin) or internal (say sensors that eventually are flushed from the system), the digital twin could collect massive amounts of data about you.

For example, what if you lost 10 pounds of fat all else being equal. Your digital twin could tell you what the impact on your overall body could be with that change—or reducing your HDL cholesterol level by 5%—or increasing your VO2 max level to improve your oxygen absorption capability. By making subtle changes in your digital twin environment, you may see the change opportunity in your medication. By introducing multiple changes, the user could observe at an accelerated pace what the "real you" could be like and take advantage of those health clues.

Imagine leveraging computer models of yourself in discussions with—your healthcare practitioner. Hyper accurate views of you can help them diagnose and hyper-personalize medication, supplement, and fitness regimes based on a data-driven digital twin.

Digital twins also provide new fitness insights for sports teams and individuals. One research team from Milan, Italy, applied software called **SmartFit** to create digital twins (DT) of athletes "tracking fitness-related measurements describing an athlete's behavior in consecutive days (e.g. food income, activity, sleep)." Once the DT collects enough data, it predicts the athletes' performance during training, offering suggestions to modify performance to optimize results. SmartFit provides teams with a framework to help coaches and trainers monitor athlete performance. Athletes use wearables and logs to gather data stored by the DT and processed ongoing, with each iteration improving the DT's predictive capability. Early results demonstrated SmartFit's computation of reliable predictions about the human twin and recommendations for optimization. What if you could walk into a fitness centre or at your own home or through your mobile app engage a digital twin to optimize your nutrition and fitness? It is coming.

One such example is funded by Japan's NTT Docomo, a telecommunications giant, investing $230 million in a Silicon Valley lab to create digital twins of people for medical research. The digital twins will provide the lab with the opportunity to conduct tests with experimental drugs or treatments without impacting the patient. Up to 50 scientists initially will be employed in the Sunnyvale, California lab. While the lab will take a phased approach, building up various systems with full functionality is expected within 5-10 years.

Digital twins movement from the manufacturing industry to human health and fitness will take some time, most probably staged as technologies converge, as privacy issues are resolved, and accuracy levels improve over time.

If you've heard about 5G, you might be wondering what it is and what 4G and its' predecessors offered. According to Ericsson, the Swedish multinational networking and telecommunications company, 1G or first-generation, offered mobile voice calls. 2G added texting. 3G introduced mobile web browsing, and 4G offered mobile web browsing, millions of apps and higher internet speeds.

5G or fifth-generation telecommunications, being introduced in earnest in major markets globally in 2020, promises to be different.

While 5G operates on existing smartphone frequencies, Wi-Fi and satellite communications, you need a 5G enabled/compatible smartphone to run its applications. 5G promises to download entire HD movies in seconds and clips from YouTube instantly, eliminating time lags, faster data exchange and providing communication speeds of 1 Gigabit per second or 10x to 100x faster than 4G. Beyond those benefits, 5G can extend battery life; in fact, Samsung's new 5G compatible wearable promises a 15-day battery. Based on rumours we're hearing, we're also hopeful that the pricing of 5G smartphones and wearables like the Samsung A42 will be reduced relative to predecessors. As well, 5G offers the possibility of leaving your smartphone behind and merely using a smartwatch or other wearable without your phone being nearby; for us, smart wearable self-sufficiency translates into working out at the gym or running becoming much lighter and more flexible. If you're in a high-density population area where you've been competing for bandwidth with other wearable users, 5G offers fewer disruptions of your service.

So, what does this mean in the context of this book? Say you're in the gym, and you are tracking your performance. 5G promises to enhance your biometric readouts through increased speed and accuracy. The doctor-patient relationship will be augmented via better pipelines for digital therapeutics, VR, AR, and mixed reality to see inside the patient or client and transmit large amounts of vital data to their healthcare practitioner instantaneously. More sensors are being built into wearables, and with 5G that greater bandwidth allows for faster data exchange with the cloud and thus less local storage and better accuracy on measures like your heart rate, steps and more. If constantly charging your wearable battery, slow download and upload speeds, or potentially prohibitive costs are holding you back from extending your life and living healthier with AI, 5G may be one of your answers. We are only at the beginning of this new generation of mobile communication, and the future should be interesting to observe.

AI & BodyTech - Exoskeletons

According to a 2013 study cited by the Christopher & Dana Reeve Foundation, nearly 1 in 50 people live with paralysis – approximately 5.4 million people. Artificial intelligence has yet another role to play in people's health and fitness, particularly those who need help moving. Whether it be arms, legs or hands, exoskeletons or wearable robots are 21st-century answers to movement. Exoskeletons fit over the outside of the body and are loaded with body sensors to determine the wearer's desire in terms of movement. Over 300,000 people in the US are candidates for exoskeletons with 18,000 new candidates every year.

Several exoskeletons for paraplegic individuals include the *ReWalk Exosuit, Cyberdine's Hybrid Assisted Limbs, and Ekso Bionic's Ekso NR*. A rehabilitation clinic can now incorporate the *ReWalk Exosuit* into its operations in Europe after receiving approval. Functioning like a marionette or puppet on strings, an exoskeleton is controlled by a smartwatch combined with sensors placed on the torso to sense movements or tilts by the user resulting in the feet moving, and the suit learns using artificial intelligence

Three hundred hospitals have already leveraged the *Ekso NR* to help patients train their brains and muscles, resulting in their bodies being retrained to walk. Should barriers like cost and insurance coverage be overcome, the popularity of exoskeletons or wearable robots will increase.

157

Body wearables are expected to benefit from new thinner, lighter circuit technology increasing the comfort for the wearer. Researchers from three major global academic institutions, the National Research Institute in Rome, and the Universities of Cambridge and Surrey, for example, completed a study demonstrating how source-gated transistors (SGT) can create compact circuit blocks. These circuit blocks would be more cost-effective, reduce waste and improve the overall performance of the technology woven into lightweight and flexible wearables and sensors.

Future Smartwatches

Every day one can read about developments in smartwatches and other wearables. With the release of Apple Watch 6, Apple introduced the tag line "The future of health is on your wrist". We live that focus every day, secure in the knowledge that wearable vendors augment new versions of their products to drive *Deep Health*-type insights.

Apple Watch followers like Max Weinbach (EverythingApplePro on YouTube) suggest future that models could detect panic attacks *instantaneously*. Extending the Apple Watch capability to a users' mental health and wellbeing is not unreasonable. Based on some exciting detective work by Apple Insider, some future generation of Apple Watch will "scan the veins in your wrist and hands as a way to sense non-touch gestures." So, what are the implications of such a capability? Apple Insider suggests gesture control could be used with Apple's augmented reality glasses and for interpreting sign language gestures. The future of the smartwatch and its capabilities seem unlimited and indeed form a vital part of the *Deep Health* solution.

Digital Contact Lenses

Wearables are not restricted to the hands, arms, or skin. Eyes are incredible ground for wearable, smart contact lenses (SCL). SCL's can collect information about the wearer digitally and display outputs to another device. Smart contact lenses are lightweight, often made of hydrogel and gold, have several possible functions, and can be worn for extended periods.

Why would someone want to have futuristic contact lenses in their eyes? One purpose of SCL's is to monitor certain chronic medical conditions, including diabetes, far-sightedness, high cholesterol, glaucoma, and intraocular pressure. Teams at Purdue University, the South Korean Ulsan National Institute of Science and Technology, and Google/Novartis have all been developing smart contact lens solutions to improve the management and monitoring of the wearer's health. By combining sensors, power transfer circuits, wireless technology, and displays, smart contact lenses are becoming increasingly comfortable and functional. The 2018 MIT Sloan Healthcare Innovation Prize winner, *Theraoptix*, developed a lens that delivers medication in a controlled fashion without impacting vision clarity.

In the non-medical forum, smart contact lenses for use in augmented reality scenarios are growing. Involved with SCL's since 2016, Samsung aims to offer an improved AR experience with built-in cameras, antennas, and displays controlled by the wearers blink and other movements. One academic institution in France, IMT-Atlantique, is doing pioneering SCL work developing eye trackers with Wi-Fi capabilities that can be worn within AR helmets. Text and video images projected into the eye/contact lens's central area are the objectives of The Care Harmony Group. These capabilities, plus the Wi-Fi earbud and smart glasses, are leading to a more handsfree world.

3D Printing Your Food

One might imagine a person walking up to their refrigerator, and through a series of manual or verbal commands, request a nutritious meal uniquely styled to their physiology, optimizing their health and making their gut buddies happy. Sound like another Star trek invention (the food replicator)? Well, yet again the TV series is meeting reality through the technology advances in 3D printing.

3D food printing, a layer by layer process of manufacturing food products, has advanced substantially in the 21st century. Our readers may have heard of 3D printing of plastics, prosthetics, dental apparatuses, and even construction of buildings. I recently met with a company that produces dental mouth aligners. The manufacturing process is completed by a series of a dozen or so 3D printers and trimmers. Complete houses and apartment buildings are being 3D printed around the world. Yet what does this have to do with our subject, *Deep Health*?

Advances in 3D food printing permit users to incorporate pre-set recipes for a wide variety of foods differentiated by shape, colour, texture, flavor or nutrition and triggered remotely by their computer or smartphone. 3D printing of food is a relatively new concept with many considerations regarding safety, copyright, speed, the fragility of the food and multiple material printing. Still, 3D printers functionally can customize food by the level of sugar, vitamins, minerals, and protein we consume. One company, **Nourished 3D**, focuses on the healthcare of those who consume gummies vitamins (28 different ones) in a very personalized way. Surveys completed by users direct the 3D printer to create unique nutritional gummies for the consumer.

Dr. Rickey Yada is Professor and Academic Dean of the Faculty of Land and Food Systems at the University of British Columbia (UBC). A Vancouver native, Yada earned his BSc (Agriculture), MSc and PhD from UBC. Dr. Yada is a well-known and respected voice in the Canadian Food and Agri-Food Industry.

In 2019, Dr. Yada gave the 1867 Harraway and Sons Ltd., Visiting Professorship Lecture, at the University of Otago in NZ, where he discussed the possibilities of using 3D printing to develop fully personalized foods.

These products would fit individuals' specific nutritional needs and preferences. For example, by providing an ageing population's specific dietary needs where chewing and swallowing (dysphasia) is problematic. 3D printing will create foods that closely resemble the original source in content, form, texture, shape, flavor, aroma, and deliver specific needs, while still appealing to the consumer. He also believes that 3D printing will help manufacturers transform less appealing ingredients such as algal proteins, insects, or beet leaves to utilize their beneficial nutritional properties while making them more desirable.

KFC is developing the world's first 3D-printed chicken nuggets. According to an article written by Cody DeBos on medium.com, "KFC is partnering with a Russian company called 3D Bioprinting Solutions". The article goes on to explain that 3D Bioprinting Solutions will attempt to "replicate the taste and texture of real chicken" using a combination of chicken cells and plant material.

It is our belief that, powered by AI, 3D printing will revolutionize food production. Certainly, the future of food could be one we have never seen before.

Storing Data in DNA

To this point in the book, we have not discussed the topic of data storage to any great extent. Solving for petabytes (or millions of gigabytes) of data related to your own body and having that information sitting on a server in the cloud (remote server farms) can be daunting to those who want to protect the privacy of their data. So, is there an alternative solution?

Recent research suggests there's an alternative that's already inside you. It is millions of times more efficient than your silicon-based chip-inhabited laptop sitting on your desk or table at home. It could fit all of the world's data on just a few grams. It's your DNA.

DNA, or deoxyribonucleic acid, is composed of two polynucleotide chains that coil around each other to form a double helix. DNA carries genetic instructions related to the growth, function, and reproduction of all known organisms and many viruses. "Long after our magnetic storage becomes obsolete, nature will still be using DNA," according to Ilya Finkelstein, an associate professor of molecular biosciences at the University of Texas at Austin.

Since beginning in the 1980s, researchers have studied DNA as a possible storage medium. The primary barrier has been the number of errors, which Finkelstein's team addressed by applying a new error correction method to the 1939 movie, *Wizard of Oz*. Yes, Wizard of Oz. Other groups have encoded full tomes like Shakespeare's sonnets, Robert Frost's poems and speeches by Martin Luther King, continually improving on error rates.

Recently collaborations between Microsoft and the University of Washington resulted in complex machines to sequence and synthesize data (in one instance, 200 megabytes – the entire War and Peace) onto

DNA. In 2019 these teams developed the first DNA storage and retrieval automation. Google, IBM and government groups are also investing in DNA storage research.

DNA storage works by encoding and decoding much like a traditional magnetic hard drive but based on the four nucleotides bases—adenine (A), cytosine (C), guanine (G), and thymine (T). Not only can one store vast amounts of data on a teaspoon of DNA, but it will last for thousands of years with almost no maintenance required (beyond a cool, dark place). The downside? Errors (1 in 100 to 1000 nucleotides today) come in the form of insertions, deletions and substitutions (think 'world' turning into 'word' or 'sword'). Still, the Finkelstein team has overcome many of these challenges in their recent work.

What does this mean for today's athlete, fitness junkie, or someone who cares about their health and related data? It could be a decade away for mass-market consumers but imagine DNA storage being part of any device you're using (smartwatch, smartphone, other wearables) and keeping it with you rather than sending that data somewhere in the cloud for processing. Interesting times ahead.

Immersing in the Virtual World

Immersive reality sales, composed of virtual, augmented and mixed reality offerings, have grown in popularity in the last decade. In fact, they are predicted to reach over $800 million globally by 2025. In China, there are more than 80 million virtual reality headsets in use today. People are exploring their uses in safety training, gaming, sales training and yes, fitness.

Virtual reality or VR is the ticket for users who want to be fully immersed in an alternate reality. Computer-generated 3D images, sounds, and vibrations allow the user to take risks, learn new skills, and simply enjoy an alternate existence through headsets and wearables. Walk on the moon, journey through the jungle, or travel through Europe all from the comfort of your home.

A study authored by researchers from three British universities and published in the British Journal of Health Psychology (BJHP) suggested that VR has incredible fitness benefits. In cycling training, VR-enabled bikes project the user into a French countryside with accompanying music, and the combination increased enjoyment in training by over 25%. A 17.5% enhancement of enjoyment in other exercising was found in the study compared to no virtual reality and music. The study leveraged the "Ready Exerciser One" from Massachusetts-based developer **VirZOOM**, which is compatible with **Oculus Quest** and **Oculus Go VR** headsets. Other vendors offer similar experiences, such as **Dance Central** and **BoxVR**. In the BJHP study, users experienced more positive emotions, physical sensations, felt more energetic, focused less on the strain of cycling, and a greater sense of achievement. With all those benefits, users would be more likely to stick to a routine.

Mixed reality (MR) offers the user the opportunity to interact with a VR environment and augmented reality or AR. AR projects images into real space. MR provides the user with both settings together. Examples of MR include retail customers walking through aisles with a heads-up display, or a surgeon operating on a patient with the benefit of an MR headset offering critical patient information or visuals, or testing out the wallpaper in your home before actually buying it.

If you're an athlete looking to practice your boxing punches, tennis swings, or baseball pitches against a virtual opponent, you will be able to do this in MR in increasing quality and realistic style. Whether you're working on your fitness, jogging, or stretching, any activity can be measured and fed back to you. **Microsoft's Hololens** is an example of MR hardware and using equipment like this will mean your home gym will never be the same. As more users spend more time at home due to COVID-19, increased VR and MR use is highly likely.

The Next Generation of 'Bots' - Nanobots

Throughout this book, we have talked about wearables and how they collect your data. In the next generation, likely within the next 20 years, those sensors will be invisible to the human eye, both around us and inside us. These inconspicuous sensors will be feeding your digital twin. Many AI-powered apps function before ingesting something, such as those that take pictures of your food choices while grocery shopping. Others operate from within the body, including nanobots.

Nanobots are microscopic materials (nanomaterials) made of a variety of components intended to carry out tasks. Their purpose can be as a delivery system (delivering drugs to the right location) or as a destruction agent (i.e. killing cancer cells) or as probes to collect information.

It is this last capability that excites us. Imagine being able to regularly gather information about all parts of your body to hyper-personalize what you do to improve your health. Feeding data to your digital twin, via your laptop or smartphone, for artificial intelligence to analyse, and alert you to potential diseases or trends and make recommendations based on that data.

When you think about nanobots, they need not be metallic objects floating around your internal systems. Nanobots are composed of a variety of materials, as we stated above. Nanobots can be composed of organic material like proteins and polynucleotides or made of diamond (particularly for situations requiring strength and high performance). Silver has been used as the base of a nanobot focusing on antibacterial capabilities. Some nanobots are coated with titanium or nickel to improve propulsion.

Since the objective is not to haphazardly send nanobots into the host body (in fact, accurate targeting is critical), the shape and size of nanobots are vital as they impact their permeability, reactivity and motion throughout the host. Some nanobots have a spiral design. Some come equipped with sensors – so far, biological, optical, chemical, magnetic, mechanical and thermal have been tested in nanobots applications. For example, biological sensors use biological reactions to identify targets like specific types of cells.

If you're one of those who have had the 'I'm going to get chipped' conversation, it's incredibly complicated, philosophical and cultural. However, we won't be engaging in this topic in this book. Our purpose is to offer our readers options. Getting hyper-accurate insights into your body, combined with artificial intelligence-powered analysis and recommendations, can potentially help you optimize your health.

Quantum Computing

When 2020 began, few would have believed the global changes that have occurred due to a microscopic virus, COVID-19. Worldwide shutdowns have been commonplace, the ubiquitous use of face masks, and predictions of case numbers continuing to grow. What, in this new reality, does this have to do with a nascent technology like quantum computing? A great deal it appears.

Researching any new strain of virus can take years using traditional methods, including classical computing, on binary machines. In April

166

of 2020, Canadian company *D-Wave* offered its quantum computing capabilities for free to COVID-19 researchers. The exciting part of this offer? Exponentially faster speeds in processing data. Using quantum computing, researchers' efforts to understand the virus and its mutations accelerate as does the development of vaccines to combat the pandemic.

While the coronavirus has reportedly caused over 700,000 deaths (at the time of writing) globally, infectious diseases are responsible for over 13 million global deaths annually, based on data from the University of Virginia. According to the Association of the British Pharmaceutical Industry (ABPI), the historical average timeframe for pharmaceutical product development from drug discovery to licensing approval is 12.5 years. During that time, 5-10,000 drug candidates are whittled down to 10-20 likeliest solutions after 4.5 years, then down to 5-10 after another 2.5 years and down to 1-2 candidates within 11 years with another eight months to receive licensing approval. These are historical averages. COVID-19 patients cannot afford these kinds of timeframes for vaccines to be developed and introduced into the market.

Understanding the impact or implications of such factors as urbanization, lab research, interaction patterns, anti-microbial resistance, ecological changes, population health, and more is challenging. Data science attempts to incorporate micro and macro complexities into traditional computation techniques to progress our understanding of the field of epidemiology. Simulating pandemics and epidemics virtually using A.I., machine learning, and today's supercomputers consume vast amounts of processing power, with slower than desired results. Challenges for traditional computing capabilities arise as groups push the limits of scale and complexity in problems relating to the field of biology.

If you've followed Brian's writing, you will have learned that quantum computing is a new (in the past decade) way of computing. Rather than using the classical bit paradigm (1's and 0's, on or off states), quantum computers use something called qubits. Qubits can have two states, 1 and 0 at the same time. Quantum computers take advantage of this entangling of the states to, in highly specific cases today, achieve algorithms that are exponentially speedier than their classical counterparts. Honeywell (as of writing, the fastest quantum computer at 64 qubits) and D-Wave, IBM and Righetti, much like those manufacturers of the original personal computers and their chips, are racing for supremacy in the fastest, lest error, most cost-effective quantum computers.

Indeed, arguments occur in the press and academia that predicting the rate of future quantum computing maturity is speculative at best. Improving the number of qubits, reducing error rates for storage and operations, and enhancing quantum programming languages are tall orders, yet the rate of acceleration in 2020 has been exciting. **D-Wave**, the Canadian entity, now reports a quantum programming community of over 1,000 developers applying Q.C. to financial modeling, transportation routes, and protein folding. Its Leap2 system supports up to 10,000 variables, which can be fully connected.

At a country or government level, numerous countries have entered into quantum programmes, including the U.S. National Quantum Initiative Act 2018, the European Quantum Technologies Flagship, and the U.K.'s National Quantum Technologies Programme. With real-world application, corporate investment and government sponsorship, quantum computing's progress should accelerate even further.

Being able to aggregate vast amounts of data, whether at a population level or individual patient-level through in-presence testing or smart device tracking, is essential to an improved understanding of the coronavirus and its symptoms and effects. The challenge of how quantum computing can support the analysis of such data pools in a shorter time when combined with A.I. and other technologies offer an exciting new set of opportunities for those interested in their own *Deep Health.*

Predictions

Two years ago, I wrote that predictions for AI for 2019 were coming out fast and furious. And what were they saying? "AI will become more of a commodity, require smaller data lakes, improve its conversational capabilities, become the "other person" in your home, develop hyper-accurate diagnoses, determine who gets hired, improve life for the [disabled] and so much more." Significant progress in AI from brilliant human minds continues to push the limits of the technology.

In late 2019, I had the pleasure of watching a webinar attended by over 2,000 people worldwide, hosted by Peter Diamandis, head of Abundance Digital, featuring Ray Kurzweil. Kurzweil is the renowned American inventor, futurist and Google's Director of Engineering. Kurzweil's list of honors is too numerous to mention, though he is probably most recognized for his predictions.

Kurzweil predicted the explosion of the Internet, the computer's progress in beating humans in chess by the year 2000 (it happened in 1997), that wireless systems would become dominant, and famously that machines would pass the Turing Test by 2029 (just a decade away). That's closer in time than the original iPhone is to the iPhone 11 of today. Over a hundred of Kurzweil's predictions were accurate, which made his presentation all the more penetrating in its implications.

He opened with the implications of AI on the health sciences, in particular, radiology. He argues that today's machines are now much more accurate than doctors, and within a few years, radiologists as a role will be redundant. A machine with consciousness, emotions, and feelings are all part of his predictions for the advancement of machines. With advances leading to 10 to the 18th power computations on the cloud through neural nets, such intelligence he states is possible within the decade.

Today a computer at Google can read 120,000 books and tell you the best five responses to a question – within one second. Humans are incapable of doing that. Kurzweil says that a brain-computer interface is inevitable, certainly by the 2030s. *Neuralink*, for example, announced in late 2019, it was operating at approximately 2GB per second, but progress will be needed to achieve the human brain's speed.

Kurzweil argues that technology helps humans much more than it has the potential to hurt them. A child in Tanzania has access to the world's knowledge through their smartphone. Poverty has fallen dramatically since 1900. Food production is being generated in new, creative ways to feed the world. By the 2030s, nanotechnology will be applied to bio-science to replace organs, flow through the bloodstream correcting for diabetes and other ailments, and connecting the brains' neocortex to the cloud helping those with brain limiting issues to communicate. Additionally, leveraging AI and quantum computing, shorter testing times will introduce new medicines faster to the world's population. Thinking about the future can create anxiety and hope at the same time. Ray Kurzweil has lived that for the last 60+ years, and often, when it comes to predictions, he's right.

We think the future will be incredible. Digital twins. Nanobots that move through your body. Exoskeletons you wear to move around or pick up heavy objects. Quantum computing to process information at exponentially faster speeds. Smart contact lenses that sense your medical condition and display virtual worlds to you. The elements of *Deep Health*.

Now let's move from the possible to the actual. In the next chapter, we suggest how you can get started on your *Deep Health* journey.

Chapter 15

How to Get Started

"The miracle isn't that I finished. The miracle is that I had the courage to start"
— *John Bingham, Author and Runner*

Throughout **Deep Health**, we've spoken about our passion for fitness, health, and longevity via the data we collect about ourselves and artificial intelligence's incredible capabilities. We're so excited for you to achieve your goals through a hyper-accurate understanding of yourself.

So, now you know the data that is available, and which applications or solutions provide them. Now, how do you decide what's relevant for you, and how do you prioritize your choices?

It takes time to figure out what's right for you and to absorb these new technologies. So, it's essential to prioritize. There are many considerations so that you're not overwhelmed, and the first is to take your time. Rob & I took years to get to this point, and while we're hoping to shorten the road for you, you're going to enjoy the journey through a multitude of milestones. Take your time. Don't rush into multiple objectives all at once. You'll get overwhelmed and frustrated for not achieving your goals.

How do you think about collecting data about yourself? Can you understand what it's telling you and act on these insights within your already busy schedule? You will find as you achieve each milestone, you'll want to do even more. So enjoy each step while it's in front of you. It's fun to experience a better heart recovery rate, a higher VO2 max level, a lower BMI, or whatever you're striving for. You need to get into the routine of changing your behaviour, and any change is rarely easy. But you will find you'll accelerate towards each milestone as you pass another.

Prioritizing which app or activity you engage, will depend upon your current state. It could be that you have a mental block, and you need to focus on feeling better in your mind first before moving onto the rest of your physiology. Or maybe you are overweight and want to feel better walking up the stairs, or in those old clothes you used to wear, or as a prelude to engaging in a new activity.

Deciding whether to do this on your own or to engage with a partner, trainer, or coach could be part of your prioritization process. If you feel you need help to get going, or if you're in a class that requires you to provide data about your activities, there are many options to accommodate you. Review the options, whether those introduced here, recommended by your trainer, or through software reviews online in sites like G2, CNET or Capterra, or your favourite blog. Rob and I often compare notes on the data we're collecting, and it's even more motivating to continue as we digest what the results mean. Having a partner in this can keep you engaged and share your experiences, good or bad. While we do a lot of self-taught interaction with our smart devices we also keep each other informed on what's new and working for us.

Budget is another consideration. The newest smartwatches range from US $300-600, and smartphones can reach $1,000. On the other hand, there are numerous free apps on the Internet. Cost may stop you from jumping into too many activities at once. Try out a demo or free version. Ask your friends and acquaintances what they use. Leverage the suggestions in this book. There are many options to try without breaking the bank. Whether it's on Apple's AppStore, through Google Play or other sites, free apps can be functional without having to move on to the upgrades.

If you're experiencing a health crisis and working with a healthcare practitioner, ask them what areas you should be focusing on, and then do your research on what apps and smart technology would satisfy those needs. Early on in our journey, we pushed our doctors to tell us what we needed to do to accelerate our respective recoveries and reduce the dependence on medication. Through questions posed for crucial health points, we were able to adjust our nutrition, fitness, and mental health choices to accelerate recovery.

Family disease history could be yet another priority consideration where you could select a smart tech option. Brian's mother and her family had a history of heart disease, and his work stress, lack of fitness and poor eating habits moved that forward by decades. Knowing that in advance may prove to be a deciding factor for you to choose a related app.

These are just some of the factors you might consider when selecting your next steps on the road to *Deep Health*. Don't let it be daunting. Take your time. Gain some wins. Then think about these next steps.

Steps:

1. *Go deep into your focus areas.* Do your research about your health issue or your fitness goal. Get involved in what the experts are saying about your topic. Go deep. Talk to others. Feel the issue in new terms that give you hope for change.

2. *What data makes up that focus?* Accept that there are many experts with varying opinions. When Rob and I debate the merits of each expert's approach, we realize there are facts to support each of their positions, but none of those experts know you and your situation. If you are a vegetarian who has irritable bowel syndrome, you are not inclined to eat certain legumes or beans, yet vegetarian diets call for them. Find those experts you trust through their books, websites, articles or blogs and weigh their advice against others you respect.

3. *What do I want to do with that data?* You have a goal in mind. Decide on how the information you've collected can help you towards that goal. When Brian first got his T2 diabetes diagnosis, he knew very little about the disease despite the family connection. So he jumped into researching the causes and the implications for changes in diet, fitness, and more.

4. *What options do I have?* There are so many AI-powered options available today that were not there in the previous five years. When selecting any smart tech option, whether it is to help meet your goals, improve your focus, or help motivate you, the data you collect and what you do with it should not be

a task you take lightly or alone. Have fun discussing your options. The 21st century offers us high stress, but also great solutions to our healthspan objectives.

5. *Monitor your progress.* Whenever we connect with colleagues in the smart tech community (aka our local fitness friends), we share the latest graphs, tables, rewards, trophies, and badges produced by smart tech vendors. We also look at the trend analysis resident on our devices to see how we're progressing. Day-to-day, week-to-week, month-to-month validate the activities you're doing are contributing to your better self. Find a trusted friend or partner to share your results with – that interpersonal feedback can be highly motivating.

6. *Finally* – get started. As we opened this chapter with John Bingham's quote about it being a miracle to start, it often is when you reflect on where you are today. Achieving milestones, perceiving yourself differently and benefitting from advances in technology, including artificial intelligence, we hope you will be healthier and also be happier for the long term.

Chapter 16

Conclusion

"Keep going forward because success will come" –
Cassandra Sanford, CEO Kelly Mitchell Group

Today is merely a point in time. As we did, you have a phenomenal opportunity to leverage the power of artificial intelligence to achieve your health and fitness goals. Your success will depend upon your motivation, knowledge, use of technology, and how that technology evolves.

One day, in the not too distant future, nanobots may be streaming through your system, your digital twin could give you insights into your next meal, and your exoskeleton might help you lift that heavy rock in your garden without causing you any strain. Technology like artificial intelligence and quantum computing is racing forward. But that doesn't mean you need to be at the forefront. You can benefit today from exciting new developments that are available on your smartphone, smartwatch or other wearable devices.

The journey that Rob and I started on years ago was fraught with challenges, milestones, technology purchases, research, heated discussions, and a good deal of sweat. It was worth every step.

Perhaps you bought this book to achieve some goal. Possibly to live longer or enjoy your life right now. Whichever the reason, we hope reading this book will help you on your way. We are so passionate about the health span journey that we learn something new every day, and we push ourselves to be better than we were yesterday (sometimes that family pizza night gets in the way, but that's ok!)

By reading this book, you've demonstrated your openness to the potential of artificial intelligence in fitness and health. If you've read this far, continue reading from other sources. Make it part of your everyday activities. There is so much to know about artificial intelligence, and it's accelerating daily. Find ways to keep current, and it will pay dividends for your own life. Buckle your seat belt for what will be an incredible ride.

Brian Lenahan & Rob Kowal, Mississauga, Canada 2020

A Quick Favor Please?

Before you go may we ask you for a quick favor?
Good, we knew we could count on you.

Would you please leave this book a review on Amazon?

Reviews are very important for authors, as they help us sell more books. This will in turn enable me to write more books for you.

Please take a quick minute to go to Amazon and leave this book an honest review. We promise it doesn't take very long, but it can help this book reach more readers just like you.

Thank you for reading and thank you so much for being part of the journey.

Brian & Rob

Brian Lenahan is an Artificial Intelligence Strategist having received his Artificial Intelligence training at the Massachusetts Institute of Technology (MIT) Sloan School of Management (Cambridge, MA). During a 22-year career, including executive roles at a Fortune 500 Bank in the US and Canada, his consistent career thread has been aligning technology & business needs.

Leading multimillion-dollar programs and teams of over 150 employees in the US, Canada and partnering with resources in India, Brian understands the demands of leadership. He has experience in numerous industries, including Financial Services, Computer Services, Transportation, and Real Estate, as well as functions including Strategy, IT, HR, Operations, Learning, and Financial Crimes & Fraud Management. He has consulted with C-Suite, and Senior Management leaders for over 15 years.

Brian Lenahan is a recognized keynote speaker and a developer of AI strategies for large corporations. He is the CEO of Aquitaine Innovation Advisors (an AI consulting firm) and the Author-in-Residence of the 3,500-member AIGeeks meetup community-based in Toronto, Canada. Brian's experience skydiving, parasailing, zip-lining canyons, and running half-marathons led to his approach of balancing prudent risk-taking while still seeking out adventurous opportunities.

Brian is currently pursuing his Doctorate in Innovation & Strategy. He is the author of three previous books on artificial intelligence, Amazon bestseller "Artificial Intelligence: Foundations for Business Leaders and Consultants," "Digital Coach: Coaching in the Era of Artificial Intelligence," and "Artificial Intelligence: Transitions – How to Successfully Prepare for Career Where AI is Everywhere", all available on Amazon.ca. He currently is an Instructor at McMaster University in Hamilton, Ontario, Canada.

In 1981, **Rob Kowal** graduated from the Food & Drug Technology program at Durham College in Oshawa, Ontario. Since then, he has enjoyed a rewarding career in the Canadian Food & Beverage industry with considerable leadership experience and expertise in Product Development, Sales and Sales Management, Operations, and General Management. Before founding Kriscor & Associates in 2006, Rob worked for many well-known food ingredient companies in the Canadian Food Industry.

Rob is committed to lifelong learning, and recently completed on-line courses in Nutrition & Health: Human Microbiome; and Nutrition, Heart Disease & Diabetes from Wageningen University & Research in The Netherlands, one of the leading international universities in the field of healthy food and living environment. He also attended the Orchestrating Winning Performance program at IMD in Lausanne, Switzerland, which develop leaders who transform organizations and contribute to society.

Rob has served in various volunteer roles, including Chair of the Mississauga Board of Trade in 2005 and is the current (2019-2020) President of the Canadian Institute of Food Science and Technology.

He is an avid cyclist and nutrition advocate and speaks about food and consumer trends and best practices across Canada.

APPENDICES

Globally 16% of businesses are using AI today, which is heavily skewed towards large companies who have made significant early investments in AI. But as AI becomes increasingly commoditized, AI becomes more accessible to small and medium-sized businesses who are creating fascinating new AI-powered solutions.

AI usage differs widely by country: a 2019 PwC study showed 25% of Chinese companies widely use AI, versus only 5% in the US. Most American companies are running pilots but have yet to scale up like china and are falling behind. In Davos, Switzerland, the 2019 World Economic Forum called out AI as one of the leading change agents globally.

Finland is considered one of those most innovative countries in the world (currently 7th), according to the 2020 Global Innovation Index. The Index, which analyzes criteria using seven metrics, including research and development spending, manufacturing capability, and high-tech public companies' concentration, ranks Finland high on many of these criteria. According to "This Is Finland," the country is "making the most of artificial intelligence" and demonstrates how a country can leverage AI for its citizens, including opportunities for their health. The Finnish government plays a role in Finland's AI ecosystem by making it easier for businesses to exploit artificial intelligence and leverage data analytics' magic based on citizens' major life events to build predictive services. The government sees this as a way to remain competitive internationally and sustain growth in the Finnish economy. The Ministry of Economic Affairs and Employment of Finland offers an Artificial Intelligence program with subgroups focused on Competence and Innovations, Transformation of Society and Work, Data and Platform Economy, and Ethics, with documentation including news, blog posts, reports, and press releases.

One Finnish AI start-up, IrisAI, developed a science R&D assistant that's AI-powered and supports searching for relevant research papers without specific keywords. Inside the field of EdTech, there's Claned Group. Personalized everything is the way of the future, and personalized learning is no different. The Claned Groupaligns the best of artificial intelligence, data analytics, and Finnish educational expertise to offer a "personalized online learning platform." Such personalized platforms will serve users in their *Deep Health* aspirations in learning over time.

According to the Swedish Trade & Invest Council, the Swedish government believes artificial intelligence will enhance the country's competitiveness and overall welfare, so it has prioritized its development. Joining with other Nordic and Baltic nations affords an opportunity for the region to make it an AI superpower. In fact, according to a 2017 European Commission survey, 80% of Swedes feel positive about AI and advanced robotics. The majority of the population in North America have a somewhat grimmer view of AI akin to the Terminator hype.

Universities in Sweden, like KTH Royal Institute of Technology, Chalmers University of Technology, Linköping University, and Lund University, are involved in Sweden's most extensive individual research program called Wallenberg AI, Autonomous Systems and Software Program (WASP). WASP focuses on self-driving vehicles, including trucks from truck-maker Scania, machine learning, and other software, bringing 200 students into the AI arena within the decade.

The Swedish AI Council has a very attractive mission statement that focuses on what I talk consistently about in my presentations – namely, #aiforgood. Specifically, they say, "The AI Council's mission is to create a Swedish model for artificial intelligence (AI). The Swedish model for AI will be a sustainable model beneficial to society and promoting long-term economic growth." Clean green (carbon neutral) energy projects and new sustainable data centers being built by Microsoft form part of the future AI platform in this progressive country.

Whenever I speak to groups about artificial intelligence, inevitably, a question arises from the audience about the safety, or contrarily, the risk of AI. Much like any other part of our society, we need regulators to provide oversight. The following represents just some of the issues companies will want AI regulators to address sooner rather than later.

a. The knowledge that regulators can keep pace in this era where machines learn, so they change

b. Focus on regulations performance rather than command and control, which won't keep pace with AI research, creativity, and implementation

c. Business councils that drive best practices

d. AI tools (such as Reg-Tech) that do red-flagging compare public regulations against a companies' development paradigm and their internal policies.

e. Penalties that correspond with rationality

f. Dealing with multiple AI regulatory bodies within one geography. Will one body override or be the appeal body for others (The Feb. 11 Executive order in the US, the Office of Management & Budget to issue guidance for other regulatory bodies) or National Institute of Standards and Technology? For example, current regulators:

g. FDA currently regulates machine learning (ML) in medical devices

h. FAA regulates aerospace parts using generative design

i. National Highway Traffic & Safety Administration regulating self-driving cars

j. Dealing with AI regulatory bodies in multiple geographies – for example, the US issued its Executive Order in February 2019. Canada has yet to define any real AI regulatory process, let alone clear regulations.

k. Open source standard tools for bias assessment (like IBM's)

l. An efficient algorithm assessment process – fast reviews by regulators to not slow down the innovation and productivity of AI development

m. Aligning of public regulation with the increasing call for "Responsible AI" standards

n. A reasonable prioritization of regulations – don't focus on AI research first, instead focus on applications that impact social order/consumer first.

o. Address the changing view of harm, as in the case of self-driving cars causing fewer overall accidents than human-driven cars but being called out for even a single accident. Addressing the standard regulation issue – the greater the amount of regulation, the greater potential for slower AI development, lesser creativity, higher penalty potential.Standards for explainable AI (the black box issue) so that companies don't have to revisit each time.

Why should our readers care about AI both for themselves?

- If you care about remaining healthy or achieving health
- If you care about being efficient with your activities
- If you care about functioning in an environment where you understand how to optimize your use of AI
- To the extent you aren't embracing it now, you're slowing down the ability to continue to scale your health & fitness efforts

How can you prepare yourself to leverage AI?

- Understand AI, not from technical programming or coding perspective, instead of from a use case perspective.
- Use AI in your daily practices.
- AI is in every industry (notwithstanding some are slower than others), so every person who wants to supercharge their efforts needs to understand where new AI solutions are coming from.

What are the biggest mistakes or missteps that people make around AI, and what are they missing out on?

- Trying to do too much. It's good to have big plans over the long term, but critical to focus your efforts in the short term.
- Missing the boat. The difference with being in the AI world is it grows exponentially faster than anything we've seen in the past.

The Hype - AI is a prime example of how technology can be hyped in the media. So it's essential to understand what's real and what's potential.

AI can be segmented by function including machine learning, decision making, natural language processing, responding, computer vision and hearing:

- Machine Learning (ML) can include recommendation engines (like Netflix), data mining, deep learning, reinforcement learning, supervised and unsupervised learning. Machine Learning is the science of enabling computers to learn and act like we do, learning over time, on their own (autonomously) much the way we do. Humans learn through stories, facts, memory, and experiences. Computers take in data (historic pictures of dogs and cats for example) and then through ML form conclusions (it's a cat or a dog).

- Deep Learning is a subset of ML where algorithms leverage those neural networks we spoke about earlier (in this case the digital kind). Given some early success with deep learning, it is increasingly a preferred way to train computers especially where the activities are complex and have extremely large data sets. Mimicking the human brain to some shallow degree, deep learning learns through trial and error much like animals do.

- Deep Neural Networks are actually quite simple. You pose a question like is the animal in this picture a cat or a dog. By starting with an input layer of millions of images of dogs and cats injected into an algorithm, processed millions of times, there is an output layer with a probability factor that this is a dog or a cat.

- Supervised Learning – Where data can be labeled, this is an effective way for a machine to learn a function from labeled training data.

- Unsupervised Learning – Most of the world's data (over 90%) has been produced in the last two years, and most of that data is unstructured (in other words not labeled) so a different approach to training computers was required. Unsupervised learning draws

190

inferences from datasets finding hidden patterns or grouping in data.

- Cognitive Computing – often used as a synonym for AI, is slightly different in that it generally provides information for a human to solve a problem and stops short of providing the solution itself. The concepts overlap in many ways, however, as cognitive computing is based on the simulation of human processes in a computerized model. Like AI, it involves self-learning systems that use data mining, pattern recognition, and natural language processing

  - Classification – this process allows computers to understand to which category a piece or set of data belongs.

  - Regression – A statistical technique for estimating the relationships among variables (includes linear regression, logistic regression, and other approaches)

  - Algorithm – A self-contained step-by-step set of operations to be performed. Algorithms perform calculation, data processing, and/or automated reasoning tasks.

  - Decision-Making – can include case-based reasoning and expert systems

  - Computer Vision (CV) and hearing – includes facial & gesture recognition, handwriting recognition, optical character recognition, image & video recognition, and speech recognition. CV attempts to optimize the vision capability of a computer or machine. It takes one or more images and enhances information extraction from them.

  - Natural Language Processing or NLP – includes natural language understanding, programming. sentiment analysis and machine translation. NLP gives computers the ability to comprehend human speech, whether written or spoken. The most well-known examples today are Apple's Siri, Google assistant, and Amazon's Alexa. Another example is the ability to summarize a set of documents (this is one of my favourites as a consummate researcher and curiousity geek). NLP permits review of millions of documents, and natural language generation can then create summary reports from all of that information. Potara is a multi-document summarization system that uses NLP.

- Robotics – often used in dangerous environments like bomb detection, manufacturing, or space exploration, robots can simply be automation or can take human form helping the acceptance of a robot in activities usually performed by people. Robots can replicate walking, lifting, speech, cognition, and more as advances are made.

Age	Employment status
Height	Education level
Weight	Family Income
Blood Pressure	Sleep duration
Cholesterol	Major Stressors
HDL	Financial Stress
Personal opinion on Health	Social partnerships
Health problems	Do you like your life?
Asthma?	Where you live
Diabetes?	Encouragement from others on health
Tobacco use	Encouragement from others on energy
Second-hand smoke	Learning new things everyday
Alcohol use	Improving the area where you live
Aspirin intake	Feeling active/productive
Cancers?	Speed of walking
Heart-attack?	Time doing aerobic exercise
Stroke?	Time doing weight training
Therapy for depression	Time sitting per ay
Chronic pain	Servings of fruit
Dental Visits	Servings of vegetables

Colon Cancer Check	Servings of dairy
Flu Vaccine	How much soda
Pneumonia Shot	How much nuts
Medication for Mood	How much processed food
Taking Medication as Prescribed	How much vitamin D
Keeping Medical appointments	How often you wear a seat belt
Relationship status	Does vehicle have air bags
Relationship happiness	Do you smoke
Number of people in household	Ethnic background

Body Mass Index
Body Fat Percentage
Fat-free Body Weight
Subcutaneous Fat (the fat under your skin)
Visceral Fat (the fat around your organs)
Body Water Percentage
Skeletal Muscle Percentage
Muscle Mass
Bone Mass Percentage
Protein Percentage
Basal Metabolic Rate (minimum energy needed)
Metabolic age

Active energy - calories burned over and above metabolic rate (natural sitting burn rate)
Blood Pressure – manually entered
Body Fat %
BMI
Caffeine levels
Cycling distance (any activity)
ECG (watch)
Environmental Sound levels (7-day exposure)
Exercise minutes
Flights of stairs climbed
Food intake (dietary energy)
Headphone audio levels
Heart rate (beats per minute)
Height
High Heart Rate Notifications
Low Heart Rate Notifications
Lean Body Mass Mindful Minutes
Fall detection
Resting energy
Resting heart rate
Sleep analysis (duration, REM, deep, active)

Standing hours (ie every hour, for how long)
Number of steps taken
Nutrition intake ((proteins, vitamins, minerals)
Swimming distance
V02 max
Water level (drinking)
Weight
Workout (duration of workout)

Vendor	Offering
Babylon Health	Babylon Health is based in the United Kingdom and known for their remote consultation service. The free smartphone app utilizes A.I. matching users to a relevant physician based on their concerns, 24/7, through video or voice call. Deep learning also gives Babylon's A.I. system the ability to provide users with personalized health suggestions. Babylon Health has already introduced their app to Rwanda and select British cities, with plans, as of writing, to expand in the US, Middle East and China.
Atomwise	Founded in San Francisco, Atomwise's goal is to reduce med dev costs through advance prediction of success of potential medicines. The firm's AtomNet leverages convolutional neural networks, used in autonomous vehicles, to generate accurate predictions regarding the binding of small molecules to proteins to identify effective and safe drug candidates.
iCarbonX	Digitizing human life is the objective of this Chinese company collecting sample data including air quality, saliva, diets, and fitness activities to create a "digital you" based on your unique data. iCarbonX has designated their A.I. technology to search through individual's data to detect signals about longevity, health, and disease leading to product offerings personalized to the users' needs.
Buoy Health	With their A.I. technology, Buoy Health uses different algorithms to diagnose and treat illness. Patient's share their health concerns and symptoms to a chatbot that will guide them to the correct cure based on its diagnosis. Buoy Health is already being used by many hospitals and healthcare providers, including Harvard Medical School.
BioXcel Therapeutics	Named as one of the "Most Innovative Healthcare AI Developments of 2019", BioXcel Therapeutics utilizes A.I. to develop new medicines in the immuno-oncology and neuroscience fields. The company has also created a drug re-innovation program that uses A.I. to find new applications for

	existing drugs and identify new patients.
Deep Genomic	It is statistically proven that finding the right candidates during a drug's development raises the chances of successfully passing clinical trials, while decreasing time and cost to market. Deep Genomics' AI platform responds to this need by finding candidates for developmental drugs related to neuromuscular and neurodegenerative disorders.
BenevolentAI	With the objective to get proper treatments to patients, when they need it, BenevolentAI uses A.I. coupled with deep learning to produce a better target selection and provide previously undiscovered insights. BenevolentAI has also partnered with major pharmaceutical groups and charities to license drugs and develop easily transportable medicines for rare diseases.
Cleveland Clinic	This world-renowned hospital has partnered with IBM to use A.I. in order to simplify the patient experience. By linking A.I. with data collection to gather information on trillions of administrative and health record data points, Cleveland Clinic is helping to personalize healthcare on an individual basis.
Tempus	The goal of this company is to utilize A.I. to help physicians identify treatments and cures, by sifting through the world's largest collection of clinical and molecular data to personalize healthcare treatments. Tempus is developing A.I. tools that collect and analyze various types of data, from genetic sequencing to image recognition. Their current focus is on A.I. driven cancer research and treatments.
Google's DeepMind Health AI	Google's software is being used by global hospitals to help move patients from testing to treatment more efficiently. Doctors can use the DeepMind Health program to collect symptoms of patients and store them in a massive data library. This helps doctors with the diagnosis stage by sifting through the dataset for comparable symptoms. In addition, the platform also notifies doctors when a patient's health deteriorates.

Note: The authors do not endorse any of the products or services that appear in this book, rather they are directional suggestions for the reader to support their own choices.

Symple Symptom Tracker	This healthy lifestyle app gives you the ability to track how you feel, sleep and eat to fully monitor your own health easily and efficiently in one application.
Drugs.com Medication Guide	This app has a complete A to Z listing of drug information online, which users can navigate through using a quick search function, enabling individuals to maintain their own medication records.
My Diet Coach	My Diet Coach is a healthy lifestyle app that helps users to reach their fitness goals with the help of their own virtual fitness coach. With features like a panic button for food cravings and inspiring tips and quotes, this app will help keep you motivated and on the right track to your goals.
Lumosity	This app is perfect for anyone who wants to keep their brain in shape with free daily brain-training games centered around critical thinking, memory and problem-solving skills.
Elevate	Elevate is another brain training program that makes personalized adjustments for each individual the more you use it. This app includes daily brain games to help improve transferable skills, like your speaking abilities and math skills.
Sleep Cycle	Sleep cycle is an app dedicated towards improving your sleep cycle through the use of an A.I. Alarm clock. This app offers a variety of features to help individuals get a healthy sleep each night including a customizable wake-up window and detailed statistics about your sleep pattern.
HealthTap	HealthTap is a great platform to use for individuals inquiring about their health. You can use the app to either ask your own personal health question to receive an answer from a doctor, or you can browse through more than 2.6 million already

	answered questions on 850 different conditions.
First Aid	The American Red Cross has designed this app to help individuals be prepared for accidents and emergencies. Not only is this app fully integrated with 911 to receive help when you need it, but it also provides instructions and videos to guide you through first-aid scenarios.
MyFitnessPal	This is another fitness app that uses A.I. to help individuals track their progress related to their fitness goals. After entering your personal info, the app can help you identify proper fitness goals personalized for you and allows you to track your diet and workout plans. In addition, individuals can connect with others in the MyFitnessPal community for extra motivation or advice.
ShopWell	ShopWell is a mobile app created to help you curate the perfect diet plan personalized to your needs and goals, while providing easy and efficient ways to follow your diet plan. The app includes features such as personalized nutrition scores when you scan a label and food recommendations, helping you find the best foods for your diet plan.
Record	Created by Under Armour, Record is a health and fitness app that provides users the ability to track your sleep, fitness, activity, and nutrition all in one place. Along with this, Record allows users to easily connect and sync devices, provides you with personalized health tips and has a community you can connect with on the app.
Lark	Lark is a mobile health app that provides you with your own personal coach, by your side 24/7. Using A.I. and health monitors, the app not only tracks various aspects of your health, including sleep and medication, but it will also text you motivational messages, just like a real-life fitness coach.

HealthifyMe	Ria is this app's A.I. powered virtual nutritionist, designed to help users with their fitness and nutrition questions through audio and text messages. This app can be used by individuals around the globe, as it can be translated into more than ten different languages.
Nutrino	Nutrino's goal is to become the leading source of nutrition information. The app utilizes NLP and mathematical models from the optimization theory and predictive analysis using API and SDK integrations to provide partners with nutrition-based data services and analyses.
FitGenie	FitGenie incorporates the use of A.I. to generate personalized data related to calorie intake, to provide users with food suggestions. The app will help you adjust your macronutrients according to the data it collects, offering a highly customized nutrition plan.
Calorie Mama	This app assists you in tracking your dietary plan using A.I. and image classification technology to identify what you are eating and how many calories it contains, with just a quick picture. Calorie Mama is the most culturally diverse food identification app on the market, as it's A.I. technology, called Food AI API is equipped to identify different dishes from across the world,
Bite AI	BiteAI is another online platform that uses A.I. and image recognition to track your diet over time and identify trends in your eating habits. Machine learning enables this app to incorporate key features that make tracking your diet more efficient. For instance, the app can identify past meals, along with recognizing specific dishes and ingredients being used .

NOTES

Brown, Shelby. "120 million workers will need to be retrained due to AI, says IBM study - But many CEOs tell IBM they don't have the resources needed to close the skills gap brought on by emerging technologies." CNET. Sept. 6, 2019. https://www.cnet.com/news/120-million-workers-will-need-to-be-retrained-because-of-ai-says-ibm/

Grace, Katja, et al. "Viewpoint: When Will AI Exceed Human Performance? Evidence from AI Experts." Journal of Artificial Intelligence Research, vol. 62, July 2018, pp. 729–754., www.jair.org/index.php/jair/article/view/11222/26431.

Gagne, J.F. "Global AI Talent Report 2019" https://jfgagne.ai/talent-2019/

Chapter 1

Staff. "Chronic Disease Prevention Alliance of Canada 2018 pre-budget submission to the House of Commons Standing Committee on Finance" August 4, 2017 https://www.ourcommons.ca/Content/Committee/421/FINA/Brief/BR9 073636/br-external/ChronicDiseasePreventionAllianceOfCanada-e.pdf

Waters, Hugh; Graf, Marlon. "The Costs of Chronic Disease in the U.S." August, 2018. https://milkeninstitute.org/reports/costs-chronic-disease-us

Staff. "Centers for Medicare & Medicaid Services, 'NHE Fact Sheet'," February 20, 2019. https://www.cms.gov/Research-Statistics-Data-and-Systems/Statistics-Trends-and-Reports/NationalHealthExpendData/NHE-Fact-Sheet

Wise Old Sayings. https://www.wiseoldsayings.com/nutrition-quotes/#ixzz6KAIwbOrs

Staff. "Most Diets Don't Work for Weight Loss After a Year: Here's Why" https://www.healthline.com/health-news/diets-work-for-one-year

Zimmerman, Edith. "There's No Such Thing As a Universal Diet". The Cut. April 10, 2019. https://www.thecut.com/2019/04/how-can-artificial-intelligence-affect-diet.html

Ireland, Nicole. "Why a top Canadian obesity expert doesn't use BMI - Body mass index has been around for years, but has limited usefulness, health experts say" CBC News. Feb 23, 2020 https://www.cbc.ca/radio/whitecoat/the-dose-should-you-worry-about-your-bmi-1.5471278

Dzau, Victor; Balatbat, Celynne. "How to make later life happy, healthy and meaningful". World Economic Forum. Jan. 20, 2020. https://www.weforum.org/agenda/2020/01/a-road-map-for-healthy-longevity/

Cockrell Skinner, Asheley; Ravanbakht, Sophie N.; Perrin, Eliana M.; Armstrong, Sarah C.; Skelton, Joseph A.; "Prevalence of Obesity and Severe Obesity in US Children, 1999–2016" PEDIATRICS Volume 141, number 3, March 2018:e20173459 https://pediatrics.aappublications.org/content/pediatrics/early/2018/02/22/peds.2017-3459.full.pdf

Carroll, Aaron E. "Childhood Obesity Is a Major Problem. Research Isn't Helping. - Something is missing with many study methods." New York Times. Jan. 20, 2020. https://www.nytimes.com/2020/01/20/upshot/childhood-obesity-research.html

American Heart Association News. "How much does your doctor actually know about nutrition? May 3, 2018. https://www.heart.org/en/news/2018/05/03/how-much-does-your-doctor-actually-know-about-nutrition

Cockrell-Skinner, Asheley; Ravanbakht, Sophie, N; Perrin, Eliana, M. "Prevalence of Obesity and Severe Obesity in US Children, 1999–

2016" Pediatrics Volume 141, number 3, March 2018:e20173459
https://pediatrics.aappublications.org/content/pediatrics/early/2018/02/
22/peds.2017-3459.full.pdf

Cecchini, Michele. "Heavy Burden of Obesity: The Economics of
Prevention - A quick guide for policy makers" OECD Public Health,
Health Division. 2019. https://www.oecd.org/health/health-
systems/Heavy-burden-of-obesity-Policy-Brief-2019.pdf

MarketsandMarkets. "Smart Clothing Market by Textile Type, Product
Type, End-User Industry and Geography – Global Forecast to 2024"

Moore, Jason H., Raghavachari, Nalini. "Artificial Intelligence Based
Approaches to Identify Molecular Determinants of Exceptional Health
and Life Span-An Interdisciplinary Workshop at the National Institute
on Aging". Frontiers in Artificial Intelligence. 06 August 2019
https://www.frontiersin.org/articles/10.3389/frai.2019.00012/full

Dzau, Victor; Balatbat, Celynne. "How to make later life happy,
healthy and meaningful". World Economic Forum. Jan. 20, 2020.
https://www.weforum.org/agenda/2020/01/a-road-map-for-healthy-
longevity/

Staff. "Prevalence of Chronic Diseases Among Canadian Adults". Data
from the Canadian Chronic Disease Surveillance System (CCDSS),
2015-2016 except where noted. 2017.
(https://www.canada.ca/en/public-health/services/chronic-
diseases/prevalence-canadian-adults-infographic-2019.html)

Ramirez, Yusilla; Moore, Tamara. "Teens with obesity find artificial
intelligence coach helpful in weight-loss program - 'Chatbot' feasible
and useful in behavioral counseling of obese and pre-diabetic
adolescents." American association for the Advancement of Science.
16-MAY-2019. https://www.eurekalert.org/pub_releases/2019-05/n-
two051619.php

LaRosa, John. "Top 9 Things to Know About the Weight Loss
Industry". MarketResearch.com. March 6, 2019
https://blog.marketresearch.com/u.s.-weight-loss-industry-grows-to-
72-billion

Center for Disease Control. "Childhood Obesity Facts - Prevalence of Childhood Obesity in the United States" https://www.cdc.gov/obesity/data/childhood.html#Prevalence

Moore, Jason H.; Raghavachari, Nalini. "Artificial Intelligence Based Approaches to Identify Molecular Determinants of Exceptional Health and Life Span-An Interdisciplinary Workshop at the National Institute on Aging", Frontiers in Artificial Intelligence. Aug, 6, 2019. *https://www.frontiersin.org/articles/10.3389/frai.2019.00012/full*

Batra, Neal; Betts, David; Davis, Steve. "Forces of change - The future of health". Deloitte. https://www2.deloitte.com/us/en/insights/industry/health-care/forces-of-change-health-care.html?icid=dcom_promo_featured%7Cus;en

Rejcek, Peter. "Why AI Will Be the Best Tool for Extending Our Longevity" SingularityHub. Dec 08, 2019 https://singularityhub.com/2019/12/08/why-ai-will-be-the-best-tool-for-extending-our-longevity/

Kings College London, "AI for Longevity Summit", 12 November 2019. https://www.kcl.ac.uk/events/ai-for-longevity-summit

Dzau, Victor; Balatbat, Celynne. "How to make later life happy, healthy and meaningful". World Economic Forum. Jan. 20, 2020. https://www.weforum.org/agenda/2020/01/a-road-map-for-healthy-longevity/

Chapter 2

Staff of US National Academy of Medicine. "Heathy Longevity – Global Grand Challenge". https://nam.edu/initiatives/grand-challenge-healthy-longevity/

Dzau, Victor; Balatbat, Celynne. "How to make later life happy, healthy and meaningful". World Economic Forum. Jan. 20, 2020. https://www.weforum.org/agenda/2020/01/a-road-map-for-healthy-longevity/

The Myth of Diagnosis https://drhyman.com/blog/2018/05/04/the-myth-of-diagnosis/

Rea, Irene Maeve. "Genes vs lifestyle: what's the key to longevity?" World Economic Forum. 29 Feb 2016 https://www.weforum.org/agenda/2016/02/genes-vs-lifestyle-whats-the-key-to-longevity

Staff. "Leveraging AI To Accelerate Precision Health For Longevity" Forbes - COGNITIVE WORLD Nov 24, 2019 https://www.forbes.com/sites/cognitiveworld/2019/11/24/leveraging-ai-to-accelerate-precision-health-for-longevity/#77fa5235267e

Colangelo, Margaretta. "Introducing Longevity Industry 1.0" LinkedIn. October 29, 2019 *https://www.linkedin.com/pulse/introducing-longevity-industry-10-margaretta-colangelo/*

Moore, Jason H., Raghavachari, Nalini. "Artificial Intelligence Based Approaches to Identify Molecular Determinants of Exceptional Health and Life Span-An Interdisciplinary Workshop at the National Institute on Aging". Frontiers in Artificial Intelligence. 06 August 2019 https://www.frontiersin.org/articles/10.3389/frai.2019.00012/full

Kazumi Nishikawa. "How to get ageing populations to invest in their health – Japan". WEF. Dec. 27, 2019. *https://www.weforum.org/agenda/2019/12/ageing-population-healthcare-needs*

Foley, Katherine Ellen. "Here's how we can prepare for an aging population" World Economic Forum. Feb. 3, 2020. *https://www.weforum.org/agenda/2020/02/population-growth-high-demand-caregiving/*

Desjardins, Jeff. "This animation shows China and India's populations are ageing at different rates" World Economic Forum. January 30, 2020. https://www.weforum.org/agenda/2020/01/demographics-china-india-diverging/

Ritchie, Hannah. "The world population is changing: For the first time there are more people over 64 than children younger than 5" Our World in Data.org, May 23, 2019
https://ourworldindata.org/population-aged-65-outnumber-children

Esteban Ortiz-Ospina and Max Roser (2020) - "Global Health". Published online at OurWorldInData.org. Retrieved from: 'https://ourworldindata.org/health-meta' [Online Resource]

Rejcek, Peter. "Why AI Will Be the Best Tool for Extending Our Longevity" SingularityHub. Dec 08, 2019
https://singularityhub.com/2019/12/08/why-ai-will-be-the-best-tool-for-extending-our-longevity/

Statistics Canada. "Health characteristics, annual estimates" Table: 13-10-0096-01 - formerly CANSIM 105-0508.
https://www150.statcan.gc.ca/t1/tbl1/en/tv.action?pid=1310009601

Staff. "Health Status of Canadians 2016 – A Report of the Chief Public Health Officer". Public Health Agency of Canada.
https://healthycanadians.gc.ca/publications/department-ministere/state-public-health-status-2016-etat-sante-publique-statut/alt/pdf-eng.pdf

Haiminen, Niina; Carrieri, Anna-Paola; Kim, Ho-Cheol. "AI Can Predict your Age Based on Your Microbiome". IBM. February 11, 2020 https://www.ibm.com/blogs/research/2020/02/ai-predict-age-based-on-microbiome/

Zhavoronkov, Alex; Mamoshina, Polina."Deep Aging Clocks: The Emergence of AI-Based Biomarkers of Aging and Longevity" Cell.com July 03, 2019 DOI:https://doi.org/10.1016/j.tips.2019.05.004 https://www.cell.com/trends/pharmacological-sciences/fulltext/S0165-6147(19)30114-2

Chapman, Adam. "How to live longer: Eat this more than four times a week to lower risk of early death" The Express. May 11, 2020 https://www.express.co.uk/life-style/health/1280258/how-to-live-longer-longevity-chilli-peppers-heart-disease-stroke

Ben Yehuda, Anna. "Uber Eats reveals the most popular takeout orders in 35 U.S. states" April 7 2020, Timeout.com https://www.timeout.com/usa/news/uber-eats-reveals-the-most-popular-takeout-orders-in-35-u-s-states-040720

Spritzler, Franziska "14 Simple Ways to Stick to a Healthy Diet" Heathline. April 17, 2019 https://www.healthline.com/nutrition/14-ways-to-stick-to-a-diet#section4

Wood, Janice. "New Study Shows How Motivation Affects Diet" Psych Central. 17 Mar 2019 https://psychcentral.com/news/2019/03/17/new-study-shows-how-motivation-affects-diet/143725.html

Coldewey, Devin. "Is that supplement safe to take? This AI tool scours research to find out". Techcrunch. September 19, 2019 https://techcrunch.com/2019/09/19/is-that-supplement-safe-to-take-this-ai-tool-scours-research-to-find-out/

Schultz, Hank. "The coming revolution of AI in dietary supplements". Nutraingredients. 26-Apr-2019 https://www.nutraingredients-usa.com/Article/2019/04/26/From-the-editor-s-desk-The-coming-revolution-of-AI-in-dietary-supplements

Wiggers, Kyle. "Supp AI uses machine learning to identify supplement interactions". Venture Beat. September 19, 2019. https://venturebeat.com/2019/09/19/supp-ai-uses-machine-learning-to-model-supplement-interactions/

Thudia, Prem. "How AI Is Making It Easier For Healthcare Practitioners To Serve Up Nutrition To Patients". Forbes. Dec 9, 2019 https://www.forbes.com/sites/forbestechcouncil/2019/12/09/how-ai-is-making-it-easier-for-healthcare-practitioners-to-serve-up-nutrition-to-patients/#4d30100b686f

Staff. Why Artificial Intelligence? The Problem: Sickness, Suffering and Premature Death. The Solution: Artificial Intelligence. MaxLife Solution. https://www.maxlifesolution.com/why-ai/

Zhavoronkov, Alex. "The new era for AI-powered drug discovery and longevity biotechnology begins for Insilico following partnership with WuXi AppTec and others". Medium. Jun 11, 2018

https://medium.com/insilicomedicine/the-new-era-for-ai-powered-drug-discovery-and-longevity-biotechnology-begins-for-insilico-following-c93e6efab423

Staff. "Juvenescence and the Buck Institute Launch New Company to Develop Ketone Body-Based Therapeutics". Businesswire. February 04, 2019
https://www.businesswire.com/news/home/20190204005265/en/Juvenescence-Buck-Institute-Launch-New-Company-Develop

Tong, Amber. "Keto in a pill? Jim Mellon debuts anti-aging joint venture with the Buck dedicated to inducing ketosis." Endpoints News. February 4, 2019. https://endpts.com/keto-in-a-pill-juvenescence-debuts-anti-aging-joint-venture-with-the-buck-dedicated-to-inducing-ketosis/

Chapter 4

"Resting Heart Rate Table". Topend sports.
https://www.topendsports.com/testing/heart-rate-resting-chart.htm

Admin. "What Are All Those Numbers? Dec. 2, 2013.
http://dumbellfitness.com/what-are-all-those-numbers/

Staff. "Not All Gene Scores Are Created Equally". Gene Blue Print.
https://geneblueprint.com/pages/the-science

Sailesh, Adithya. "Internet of Bodies- An Overview - An interesting take on the future of bionic, embedded systems". Medium. July 5, 2019. https://medium.com/ieeekerala/internet-of-bodies-an-overview-9302579af62c

Broom, Douglas. "This wristband tells you what food to buy based on your DNA" World Economic Forum. 15 Nov 2019

https://www.weforum.org/agenda/2019/11/dna-shopping-food-diabetes-healthy-eating
newsgram.com)

Zeevi, D.; Korem, T.; Zmora, N.; Halpern, Z.; Elinav, E.; Segal, E. "Personalized Nutrition by Prediction of Glycemic Responses". Vol. 163, Issue 5, P1079-1094, November 19, 2015
https://www.cell.com/cell/fulltext/S0092-8674(15)01481-6

Walter, Zuzanna. "Growth Seen in Artificial Intelligence-Based Nutrition." Cardiometabolic Health Congress. March 18, 2019.
https://blog.cardiometabolichealth.org/2019/03/18/growth-seen-in-artificial-intelligence-based-nutrition/

Lempert, Phil. "AI Emerges as a New Tool for Fighting Food Allergies -Grocers, RDs have new way to imprint store's wellness image and keep shoppers safer." Winsight Grocery Business. Nov. 28, 2018
https://www.winsightgrocerybusiness.com/technology/ai-emerges-new-tool-fighting-food-allergies

Staff. "Zurich announces winners of its inaugural global insurtech competition" Zurich.ca Group Note. January 30, 2019.
https://www.zurich.ca/en/media/news-releases/2019/2019-0130-01

"In A 1st, Doctors In U.S. Use CRISPR Tool To Treat Patient With Genetic Disorder". NPR.org. Retrieved 2019-07-31.

"What is CRISPR and How does it work?". Livescience.Tech. Retrieved 2019-12-14.

Staff Editors. "3 Mistakes to Avoid When Shopping for a DNA Test - Your Free Guide to the Best Valued DNA Tests". Genetics Digest.com Undated.
https://geneticsdigest.com/best_ancestry_genealogy_dna_test/index.html?gclid=Cj0KCQjw9tbzBRDVARIsAMBplx-GYES6XQpbtOfoOAEvtJmkPLQNphgD6NRzNLgLYGN_fpjSIoE7o5MaApOrEALw_wcB

Chapter 5

Pennic, Jasmine. "Canadian Government Awards $49M Grant to Establish Canada-wide AI Health Data Platform" 05/28/2019 https://hitconsultant.net/2019/05/28/canadian-government-awards-49m-grant-to-establish-canada-wide-ai-health-data-platform/#.XnP7ES0ZNQK

Asokan, Akshaya. "5 AI-Powered Nutrition Apps that Help Fitness Enthusiasts with Their Calorie Intake." Analytics India. 08/04/2019 https://analyticsindiamag.com/5-ai-powered-nutrition-apps-that-help-fitness-enthusiasts-with-their-calorie-intake/

Phaneuf, Alicia. "Latest trends in medical monitoring devices and wearable health technology" Business Insider. Jan 31, 2020 https://www.businessinsider.com/wearable-technology-healthcare-medical-devices

Mayo Clinic. "Healthy Lifestyle Fitness" https://www.mayoclinic.org/healthy-lifestyle/fitness/expert-answers/exercise/faq-20057916

Staff. "Americans Do Not Exercise Enough" Fortune. June 28, 2018. https://fortune.com/2018/06/28/americans-do-not-exercise-enough-cdc/

Staff. Participation Pulse Report. https://www.participaction.com/en-ca/resources/pulse-report

PR Newswire. "Wearable Technology Market Size is Expected to Reach USD $57,653 Millions by the end of 2022, With a CAGR of 16.2 | Valuates Reports" Feb. 10, 2020. https://www.prnewswire.com/news-releases/wearable-technology-market-size-is-expected-to-reach-usd-57-653-millions-by-the-end-of-2022--with-a-cagr-of-16-2--valuates-reports-301001809.html

Panão I, Carraça EV. "Effects of exercise motivations on body image and eating habits/behaviours: A systematic review." US National Library of Medicine. Aug. 26, 2019. https://www.ncbi.nlm.nih.gov/pubmed/31449357

Staff. "Yoga Industry Trends". Wellness Creative Co. April 29, 2020 https://www.wellnesscreatives.com/yoga-industry-trends/

Koetsier, John. "AI-Driven Fitness: Making Gyms Obsolete?" Forbes. Aug 4, 2020 https://www.forbes.com/sites/johnkoetsier/2020/08/04/ai-driven-fitness-making-gyms-obsolete/#648b5e1b2a8f

Jessen NA, Munk AS, Lundgaard I, Nedergaard M. The Glymphatic System: A Beginner's Guide. Neurochem Res. 2015;40(12):2583–2599. doi:10.1007/s11064-015-1581-6
https://www.ncbi.nlm.nih.gov/pmc/articles/PMC4636982/

Pedlar, C.R., Newell, J. & Lewis, N.A. Blood Biomarker Profiling and Monitoring for High-Performance Physiology and Nutrition: Current Perspectives, Limitations and Recommendations. Sports Med 49, 185–198 (2019). https://doi.org/10.1007/s40279-019-01158-x December 2019

Gatorade Sports Science Institute. "Blood Biomarker Profiling and Monitoring For High-Performance Physiology and Nutrition: Current Perspectives, Limitations and Recommendations." 2020. https://www.gssiweb.org/en/research/Article/blood-biomarker-profiling-and-monitoring-for-high-performance-physiology-and-nutrition-current-perspectives-limitations-and-recommendations

Jessen NA, Munk AS, Lundgaard I, Nedergaard M. The Glymphatic System: A Beginner's Guide. Neurochem Res. 2015;40(12):2583–2599. doi:10.1007/s11064-015-1581-6 US National Library of Medicine - National Institutes of Health. May 7, 2015
https://www.ncbi.nlm.nih.gov/pmc/articles/PMC4636982/

Chertok, Greg. "Exactly What to Say to Motivate Someone to Exercise – and Stick With It". US News. Feb. 4, 2019
https://health.usnews.com/health-news/blogs/eat-run/articles/2019-02-04/exactly-what-to-say-to-motivate-someone-to-exercise-and-stick-with-it

Staff. "How to Get Energy When You're Too Tired to Workout Infographic" American Heart Association. January, 2019.
https://www.heart.org/en/healthy-living/fitness/staying-motivated/how-to-get-energy-when-youre-too-tired-to-workout

Rider, Sam. "What Impact Will The Trend Towards Peloton Style Home Workouts Have On The Fitness Market?" October 30, 2018 https://www.welltodoglobal.com/what-impact-will-the-trend-towards-peloton-style-home-workouts-have-on-the-fitness-market/?utm_campaign=embodied-ai&utm_medium=email&utm_source=Revue%20newsletter

Soneja, Atul. "Artificial Intelligence in Sports: A Smarter Path to Victory". CIO.com. Jun 5, 2019. https://www.cio.com/article/3400877/artificial-intelligence-in-sports-a-smarter-path-to-victory.html

Mashinchi, Jason. "How AI Can Help Improve Sports Performance". Cambridge Design Partnership. Undated. **https://www.cambridge-design.com/news-and-articles/blog/how-ai-can-help-improve-sports-performance**

Roy, Baijayanta. "AI Augmented Sports Revolution" Medium.com. Nov 7, 2019 https://towardsdatascience.com/ai-augmented-sports-revolution-5c0727ba7004

Alger, Mackenzie. "AI & Fitness: How AI Can Help World-Class Athletes and Average Jo(e)s" Medium.com. Jul 21, 2017. https://medium.com/aspire-ventures/ai-fitness-how-ai-can-help-world-class-athletes-and-average-jo-e-s-f4d17758d7d8

Bradshaw, Luke. "Athletes Who Play These Sports Live the Longest". TheCultureTrip.com. Feb. 19, 2018.https://theculturetrip.com/europe/united-kingdom/articles/athletes-who-play-these-sports-live-the-longest/

Staff. "Which Athletes Have the Longest Life Expectancy?" Labmoate-online.com. Apr. 6, 2015. https://www.labmate-online.com/news/news-and-views/5/breaking-news/which-athletes-have-the-longest-life-expectancy/34105

Lemez S, Baker J. Do Elite Athletes Live Longer? A Systematic Review of Mortality and Longevity in Elite Athletes. Sports Med Open. 2015;1(1):16. doi:10.1186/s40798-015-0024-x https://www.ncbi.nlm.nih.gov/pmc/articles/PMC4534511/

Gatorade Sports Science Institute https://www.gssiweb.org/en/research/All

Bedford, Tom. "Now is the perfect time to buy a new fitness tracker – here's why" April 10, 2020. Techradar.com.

Van Hoojdonk, Richard. "The future of fitness: AI-based personal training". Blog. June 13, 2019. https://www.richardvanhooijdonk.com/blog/en/the-future-of-fitness-ai-based-personal-training

Meeroona. "18 Portable Health Gadgets That Can Change Your Life". Travelaway. Apr. 17, 2020. *https://travelaway.me/portable-health-gadgets/Award-Winning Teeth Whitener*

Pilkington, Ed. "Google's secret cache of medical data includes names and full details of millions – whistleblower" TheGuardian. Nov. 12, 2019.https://www.theguardian.com/technology/2019/nov/12/google-medical-data-project-nightingale-secret-transfer-us-health-information

Chapter 6

Gut Microbiota Info
https://www.gutmicrobiotaforhealth.com/about-gut-microbiota-info/

Staff. "We Are What We Eat: AI and the Human Microbiome" Micron.com Undated. https://www.micron.com/insight/we-are-what-we-eat-ai-and-the-human-microbiome

Topol, Eric. "The A.I. Diet - Forget government-issued food pyramids. Let an algorithm tell you how to eat." New York Times. March 2, 2019 https://www.nytimes.com/2019/03/02/opinion/sunday/diet-artificial-intelligence-diabetes.html

Chapter 7

Arevalo, Evelyn. "Elon Musk's Neuralink chip could open a new door for hearing abilities". Tesmanian.com. August 01, 2020 https://www.tesmanian.com/blogs/tesmanian-blog/neuralink-hearing

Matthews, Charles; Ockene, Ira; Freedson, Patty; Rodal, Milagros; Merria, Philiip; Hebert, James.
"Moderate to vigorous physical activity and risk of upper-respiratory tract infection"
https://pubmed.ncbi.nlm.nih.gov/12165677/

Ducharme, Jamie. "A Third of Americans Are Sleep-Deprived. This Technology Could Help Them Rest Easier" TIME. January 25, 2019. https://time.com/5494363/sleep-artificial-intelligence/

McKee, Charlotte. "How AI Can Help You Sleep Better". Big Cloud. 12/03/2019. https://bigcloud.io/how-ai-can-help-you-sleep-better/

Lewis, Penelope A; Knoblich, Günther; Poe, Gina. "How Memory Replay in Sleep Boosts Creative Problem-Solving". Cell.com. VOLUME 22, ISSUE 6, P491-503, JUNE 01, 2018 DOI: https://doi.org/10.1016/j.tics.2018.03.009. https://www.cell.com/trends/cognitive-sciences/fulltext/S1364-6613(18)30070-6

Kent, Jessica. "Artificial Intelligence May Boost Sleep Disorder Treatment, Diagnosis - Artificial intelligence has the potential to enhance sleep studies, improving the diagnosis and treatment of sleep disorders." Health IT Analytics. March 2, 2020. *https://healthitanalytics.com/news/artificial-intelligence-may-boost-sleep-disorder-treatment-diagnosis*

Perez, Carlos. "The Link Between Sleep and Deep Learning" Medium. May 31, 2018 https://medium.com/intuitionmachine/the-link-between-sleep-and-deep-learning-5f7d347cc789

Staff. "1 in 3 adults don't get enough sleep". Center for Disease Control and Prevention. February 18, 2016 *https://www.cdc.gov/media/releases/2016/p0215-enough-sleep.html*

Chapter 8

Sahakian, Barbara Jacquelyn; Langley, Christelle; Kaser, Muzaffe. "How chronic stress changes the brain – and what you can do to reverse the damage." The Conversation. March 11, 2020 https://theconversation.com/how-chronic-stress-changes-the-brain-and-what-you-can-do-to-reverse-the-damage-133194

Chapter 9

Barker, Jill. "Fitness: Can exercise boost your immunity? Montreal Gazette, May 10, 2020. https://montrealgazette.com/life/fitness-can-exercise-boost-your-immunity/

Staff. "Personalized blood tests can aid immunity by revealing nutritional deficiencies, notes study". NutritionInsight.com. April, 2020 https://www.nutritioninsight.com/news/personalized-blood-tests-can-aid-immunity-by-revealing-nutritional-deficiencies-notes-study.html

Calder, P.C.; Carr, A.C.; Gombart, A.F.; Eggersdorfer, M. Optimal Nutritional Status for a Well-Functioning Immune System Is an Important Factor to Protect against Viral Infections. Nutrients 2020, 12, 1181 https://www.mdpi.com/2072-6643/12/4/1181#cite

Trafton, Anne | "Artificial intelligence yields new antibiotic A deep-learning model identifies a powerful new drug that can kill many species of antibiotic-resistant bacteria." MIT News Office, February 20, 2020 http://news.mit.edu/2020/artificial-intelligence-identifies-new-antibiotic-0220

Matti, Mariam. "Fitbit data helps U.S. researchers with real-time flu predictions". CTV News. January 17, 2020. https://www.ctvnews.ca/health/fitbit-data-helps-u-s-researchers-with-real-time-flu-predictions-1.4771984

Chapter 10

Inverse.com. https://www.inverse.com/mind-body/exercise-can-rejuvenate-stem-cells

Kaminskiy, Dmitry. "A New Framework to Address Increasing Complexity in AI & DeepTech" https://www.kaminskiy.info/new-framework

Hanstock HG, Walsh NP, Edwards JP, Fortes MB, Cosby SL, Nugent A, et al. Tear fluid sIgA as a noninvasive biomarker of mucosal immunity and common cold risk. Med Sci Sports Exec. 2016;48(3):569–77.

Heaney LM, Deighton K, Suzuki T. Non-targeted metabolomics in sport and exercise science. J Sports Sci. 2017;27:1–9.

Webborn N, Williams A, McNamee M, Bouchard C, Pitsiladis Y, Ahmetov I, et al. Direct-to-consumer genetic testing for predicting sports performance and talent identification: consensus statement. Br J Sports Med. 2015;49(23):1486–91.

Sharp NC. The human genome and sport, including epigenetics and athleticogenomics: a brief look at a rapidly changing field. J Sports Sci. 2008;26(11):1127–33.

Diamandis, Peter H., Kotler, Steven. "We are nearing 'longevity escape velocity' — where science can extend your life for more than a year for every year you are alive" MarketWatch.com Feb. 25, 2020 https://www.marketwatch.com/story/we-are-nearing-longevity-escape-velocity-where-science-can-extend-your-life-for-more-than-a-year-for-every-year-you-are-alive-2020-02-24

Nevillle, Sarah. "Why big pharma sees a remedy in data and AI - Billions are being invested into mining patient records in a bid to aid drug discovery but backers are impatient" Financial Times. January 26, 2020. https://www.ft.com/content/4743d76c-af9b-11e9-8030-530adfa879c2

Matheny, Michael; Israni, Sonoo Thadaney; Ahmed, Mahnoor; Whicher, Danielle. "Artificial Intelligence in Health Care: The Hope, the Hype, the Promise, the Peril". National Academy of Medicine.

2019. https://nam.edu/wp-content/uploads/2019/12/AI-in-Health-Care-PREPUB-FINAL.pdf

Chapter 11

Thousands die from medical errors yearly, notes advocacy group https://www.rcinet.ca/en/2019/10/28/thousands-die-from-medical-errors-yearly-notes-advocacy-group/
Study Suggests Medical Errors Now Third Leading Cause of Death in the U.S.
https://www.hopkinsmedicine.org/news/media/releases/study_suggests_medical_errors_now_third_leading_cause_of_death_in_the_us

Durrell, Katherine. "Personalized nutrition amid COVID-19: Persona CEO flags "tremendous" growth opportunities". Nutrition Insight.com. May 4, 2020.
https://www.nutritioninsight.com/news/personalized-nutrition-amid-covid-19-persona-ceo-flags-tremendous-growth-opportunities.html?utm_source=ActiveCampaign&utm_medium=email&utm_content=Weekly+News+Review+%7C+Eye+health+concerns+exacerbated+amid+increased+screen+time%2C+Industry+execs+warn+%22no+pros+in+postponing+R+D%22&utm_campaign=2020-05-11+Weekly+NI+%28PLT+Health+Solutions%29

Park, Alice. "How AI Can Predict Heart Attacks and Strokes" TIME. Feb.14, 2020. https://time.com/collection/life-reinvented/5784090/ai-heart-attack-stroke/

Chapter 12

Loechner, Jack. "90% of today's data created in two years," MediaPost, December 22, 2016; Nick Routley, "Visualizing the trillion-fold increase in computing power," Visual Capitalist, November 4, 2017.

Chapter 13

Miller, Katherine. "A Fitness App with a Story to Tell: Can Narrative Keep Us Moving?" HAI Blog. July 29, 2020 https://hai.stanford.edu/blog/fitness-app-story-tell-can-narrative-keep-us-moving

Park, Gene. "Fortnite is adding bots to help new players learn." The Washington Post. September 30, 2019 https://www.arkansasonline.com/news/2019/sep/30/epic-to-add-fortnite-bots-to-help-new-p/

Heenan-Jalil, Jeff. "'Star Trek' tricorder becomes reality (and other healthcare innovations)" Meical Economics.com. November 27, 2018 https://www.medicaleconomics.com/med-ec-blog/star-trek-tricorder-

becomes-reality-and-other-healthcare-innovations

Chapter 14

Heiting, Gary. "How vision changes as you age". All About Vision. https://www.allaboutvision.com/en-ca/over60/vision-changes/

Hill, Steve. "Reversing Age-Related Vision Loss Using Cellular Reprogramming." Life Extension Advocacy Foundation. https://www.lifespan.io/news/reversing-age-related-vision-loss-using-cellular-reprogramming/

Marr, Bernard. "The Wonderful Ways Artificial Intelligence Is Transforming Genomics and Gene Editing", Bernard Marr. Nov 16, 2018. https://www.forbes.com/sites/bernardmarr/2018/11/16/the-amazing-ways-artificial-intelligence-is-transforming-genomics-and-gene-editing/#3abeb8de42c1

Yeager, Ashley. "Could AI Make Gene Editing More Accurate?" The Scientist. Apr 30, 2019 https://www.the-scientist.com/the-literature/could-ai-make-gene-editing-more-accurate-65781

Shorten G. "Artificial Intelligence and Training Physicians to Perform Technical Procedures." JAMA Netw Open. 2019;2(8): e198375. doi:10.1001/jamanetworkopen.2019.8375

https://jamanetwork.com/journals/jamanetworkopen/fullarticle/274077
4

Kharkovyna, Oleksii. "Artificial Intelligence & Deep Learning for Medical Diagnosis - On the road to better healthcare." Towards Data Science.com. Nov. 13, 2019. https://towardsdatascience.com/artificial-intelligence-deep-learning-for-medical-diagnosis-9561f7a4e5f

Sipherd, Ray. "The third-leading cause of death in US most doctors don't want you to know about" CNBC.com Feb 22 2018. https://www.cnbc.com/2018/02/22/medical-errors-third-leading-cause-of-death-in-america.html

Haughey, John; Taylor, Karen. "Medtech and the Internet of Medical Things - How connected medical devices are transforming health care". Deloitte.com https://www2.deloitte.com/global/en/pages/life-sciences-and-healthcare/articles/medtech-internet-of-medical-things.html

Davenport T, Kalakota R. The potential for artificial intelligence in healthcare. Future Healthc J. 2019;6(2):94–98. doi:10.7861/futurehosp.6-2-94 https://www.ncbi.nlm.nih.gov/pmc/articles/PMC6616181/

University of Surrey. "Simplified circuit design could revolutionize how wearables are manufactured". Tech Explore. August 3, 2020. https://techxplore.com/news/2020-08-circuit-revolutionize-wearables.html

Chandler, Simon. "Virtual Reality Makes Exercise More Enjoyable and less tiring" Forbes. June 16, 2020. https://www.forbes.com/sites/simonchandler/2020/06/16/virtual-reality-makes-exercise-more-enjoyable-and-less-tiring-study-finds/#24d8a14cc156

DeBos, Cody. "KFC is working on world's first 3D-printed chicken nuggets" Medium.com. July 22, 2020 https://medium.com/predict/kfc-is-working-on-worlds-first-3d-printed-chicken-nuggets-ef2ab2427b7

Nield, David. "Apple Watch could detect incoming panic attacks in future models - Dealing with stress and anxiety". April 13, 2020. TechRadar.com. https://www.techradar.com/uk/news/future-apple-watch-updates-could-take-care-of-your-mental-and-your-physical-health

Wallace, Jawad. "NTT spends $230 million to build hyper realistic digital twins of humans" Techbriefly.com May 21, 2020 https://techbriefly.com/2020/05/21/ntt-spends-230-million-to-build-hyper-realistic-digital-twins-of-humans/

Gutierrez B, Bermúdez CV, Ureña YRC, et al. Nanobots: development and future. Int J Biosen Bioelectron. 2017;2(5):146–151. DOI: 10.15406/ijbsbe.2017.02.00037 https://medcraveonline.com/IJBSBE/nanobots-development-and-future.html

Bloudoff-Indelicato, Mollie. "How wearable robots are helping people with paralysis walk again". CNBC. Mar 22, 2020 https://www.cnbc.com/2020/03/22/how-wearable-robots-are-helping-people-with-paralysis-walk-again.html

Fortune Business Insights. "Exoskeleton Market 2019 Global Industry Size, Segments, Share and Growth Factor Analysis Research Report 2026". Expresswire. Aug 27 2019 https://www.theexpresswire.com/pressrelease/Exoskeleton-Market-2019-Global-Share-Growth-Size-Opportunities-Trends-Regional-Overview-Leading-Company-Analysis-Forecast-To-2025_10351049

Prospero, Mike. "Forget Apple Watch 6: Apple Watch 7 could scan your veins - A new Apple Patent hints at vein tracking for gesture controls" Tom's Guide.com. July 1, 2020. https://www.tomsguide.com/news/forget-apple-watch-6-apple-watch-7-could-scan-your-veins

Neely, Amber. "Doctor credits Apple Watch for saving his life". AI Insider. July 1, 2020. https://appleinsider.com/articles/20/07/01/doctor-credits-apple-watch-for-saving-his-life

Fourie, Louis. "AI-powered contact lenses give new meaning to 20/20 vision." Fast Company. 08.20.19 https://www.fastcompany.co.za/inspiration/ai-powered-contact-lenses-gives-new-meaning-to-20-20-vision-31008219

INDEX

Manufactured by Amazon.ca
Bolton, ON

27739915R00132